THE OPPORTUNITY
OF THE
CHURCH OF ENGLAND

THE OPPORTUNITY

OF THE

CHURCH OF ENGLAND

LECTURES DELIVERED IN THE DIVINITY SCHOOL OF
THE UNIVERSITY OF CAMBRIDGE IN 1904

BY

COSMO GORDON LANG, D.D.

BISHOP OF STEPNEY

FELLOW OF ALL SOULS COLLEGE, OXFORD
AND SOMETIME VICAR OF PORTSEA

Ἐξαγοραζόμενοι τὸν καιρόν, ὅτι αἱ ἡμέραι πονηραί εἰσιν

LONGMANS, GREEN, AND CO.
39 PATERNOSTER ROW, LONDON
NEW YORK AND BOMBAY
1905

TO MY COMRADES

THE CLERGY OF EAST AND

NORTH-EAST LONDON

IN GRATITUDE FOR THEIR EXAMPLE

AND WITH PRAYER FOR

THEIR WORK

PREFACE

THE following chapters contain the lectures on Pastoral Theology delivered in the Divinity School at Cambridge in the year 1904. At the time of their delivery the lectures were taken down in shorthand, but the transcripts of them proved to be so inadequate that I have been obliged, in the midst of much pressing work, to write them out. Hence the delay in publication. Many of the phrases, digressions, and illustrations used to give point to a spoken address have been omitted, and in some places additions have been made. Lest the title should mislead any readers, let me say at once that the lectures only profess to deal with two special aspects of a very wide subject. In spite of their only too obvious imperfections, I commend whatever truth they may contain to all who love and serve the Church of England.

AMEN COURT,
 ST. PAUL'S CATHEDRAL,
  October, 1905.

SYNOPSIS OF CONTENTS

CHAPTER I

CHAPTER II

CHAPTER III

CHAPTER VII

CHAPTER VIII

CHAPTER IX

CHAPTER X

CHAPTER XI

CHAPTER XII

APPENDICES

THE OPPORTUNITY OF
THE CHURCH OF ENGLAND

CHAPTER I

INTRODUCTION

IN these lectures I am speaking primarily to men who intend to make, or have already made, the offer of their service to God in the ministry of His Church, who have received, or hope to receive, the call and the commission of the living Head of the Church to go forth and "make disciples," to bring men within the redeemed humanity. There are other men who devote themselves to the service of their fellows inspired by some ideal of their own ; but in our case we bring to that service something more than a merely personal ideal, we bring a heritage of great convictions entrusted to our care—convictions as to the supreme value to all life of certain great facts, the birth, death, and resurrection of the Son of God ; of the Presence here and

now in the world of a living Person, the Lord
and Brother of man; of the continuous gift of
His life, through the Holy Spirit, in the fellowship and sacraments of His Church. Our service
itself is accepted and authorized by its incorpora-
tion into a historic ministry, which links our work
and witness with those of the first disciples of the
Lord. Our ministry, then, is definite, but so also
is the sphere of its exercise : for most of those to
whom I speak will be or have been sent to fulfil it
in the world of England at the beginning of the
twentieth century—a world with its own special
characteristics, dangers, and opportunities. We
are to be the interpreters of Christ to our own
country and generation ; and for this end we must
know the minds of the men among whom we
work, and discern the signs of the times in which
we live. We may well apply to ourselves the
lesson of the great war through which the nation
has passed. It is not enough that an army should
be filled with enthusiasm or convinced of the
justice of its cause ; not enough that it should
be drilled, equipped, and led in accordance with
the experience gained in other wars at other times ;
it must adapt itself to the conditions of climate
and physical structure of the country in which it
is campaigning and to the special tactics of its
immediate enemy. So with us ; we have our
unchanging creed, our definite ministry of word

and sacraments ; but these must be adapted to the conditions and calls of our own day and generation. Language and methods which were suitable to the Middle Ages, or to England in the sixteenth or eighteenth or even nineteenth century, may be no longer suitable to the England of to-day. If I may vary the metaphor, we know the ship in which we are commissioned, we know the course which we have to take, but we must keep our eyes alert and vigilant for the winds and currents we shall meet. We must be ready to tack when contrary winds assail us, and make them the very opportunities for our forward course ; we must watch the favourable tides, lest we miss their strength. Certainly we need not, as some in a spirit of faint-heartedness would often counsel, lighten the ship by throwing any part of our freight of truth and order overboard ; but we have continually to adjust the sails.

The spirit and temper with which we are to go forth could not be better described than in the words of St. Paul, which I have chosen as the motto of these Lectures. You will find them in the fifteenth verse of the fifth chapter of his epistle to the Ephesians : "Look therefore carefully how ye walk, not as unwise, but as wise ; redeeming the time [or buying up the. opportunity] because the days are evil. Wherefore be ye not foolish, but understand what the will of the

Lord is." The mark of wisdom is to be circum-spect, to have a true outlook upon both the will of God and the conditions of life in which it is to be fulfilled ; to rescue the good from the bondage of evil and claim it for God, to regard the very evils of the time as opportunities given for the fulfilment of our service.[1] This is the spirit of true wisdom—a spirit which is neither forgetful of the difficulties nor faint-hearted in the face of them. It is a spirit of a true optimism, which boldly recognizes their force, but believes that they may be converted into opportunities.

I wish, then, to think with you of some of the characteristic difficulties of our own day ; they are special in their character, but not surely special in their gravity or strength. Let us at the very out-set have the courage to be thankful for the times in which it has pleased God to ask for our ministry. It is useless to sigh for other times ; the days in which there were no special trials and difficulties, what we call "the good old times," never were. There is a maxim of the great Bishop Lightfoot, of Durham, which it is always worth while to lay to heart—"The study of history is the best cordial for drooping spirits." Think of the apostolic days, of the anxieties and disappointments which pressed heavily upon the ardent spirit of St. Paul, of the catastrophes which were witnessed by

[1] See Appendix A.

St. John ; think of the days of the great persecu-
tions, when the Church seemed almost over-
whelmed by disasters ; think of the days of St.
Athanasius, when not the world only, but the
Church itself, seemed to be lost to the faith ; think
of the Middle Ages with their depressing spectacle of the ruin of great hopes and the corrup-
tion of noble institutions; think of the time of the
Reformation with its bewildering problems and
wearisome controversies ; think of England in the
eighteenth century, and the blight of indifference
and worldliness which seemed to have settled
down upon the Church ; think of the hard hearts
and deaf ears which resisted the first movement
of the Evangelical revival ; think of the ignorance,
obstinacy, and obloquy which met the efforts of
the Church in the last century to regain its true
spiritual heritage ; think of the disquiet and even
panic with which the boasts of science in the pride
of its first great conquests, and the early challenges
of Biblical criticism, were received forty or fifty
years ago.

Think of all this, and it may help us to accept
with willing and ready obedience God's choice
of the times in which we are to serve Him with
our lives. It may be that in this first quarter
of the twentieth century there is a pause, a back-
water, in the stream of national and religious life.
There may seem to be few outstanding personali-

ties, few great and inspiring causes either in Church or State. Probably, if this be our dispirited verdict, history with its wider and wiser eyes will reverse it. But, in any case, even if it be true, may we not believe that there may be movement without the inspiration of great personalities or dramatic crises? Indeed, great personalities seem to be given chiefly before widespread movements are begun, and to be withdrawn when they have gathered force and way; and if for the moment the pace of the stream seems to be arrested, it may only be because a wider space is being covered with a slower but surer progress. At least for ourselves it is enough to be sure that the times in which God has asked for our service are the times in which we can serve Him best.

It is, then, in this spirit of faith, hope, and thankfulness that I shall ask you in these Lectures to consider specially two of the characteristic evils of our time, and the ways by which they can be bought up as a great opportunity by the Church of England. They are, first, the dissolution of definite faith and custom in religion; and secondly, the indifference towards religion of the great masses of the people. We shall first attempt to understand the causes and the character of the two evils; we shall then consider the personal equipment which we need to deal rightly with them; and finally, in greater detail, some of the specific ways in which they may be overcome with good.

May God the Holy Spirit enable us in this inquiry to have "a right judgment in all things, and evermore to rejoice in His holy comfort."

CHAPTER II

THE first special difficulty belonging to the time in which your Ministry is to be fulfilled of which I wish to speak is the strength of the forces which are dissolving the traditions, customs, and habits of religion. It is a commonplace to speak of our age as one of change; probably no period in the history of the world has witnessed changes so many and so far-reaching as the century through which we have just passed. It would be equally true to describe the age as one of dissolution in the strict sense of the term. But the rapidity of the changes has hindered the thoroughness of the dissolution. The dissolving tendencies everywhere at work have had no time to produce permanent results. They have worked vaguely and confusedly, scattering rather than uprooting, creating a general superficiality and instability of mind and character. Thus in the sphere of religion, those elements which stand upon the outer surface of life, its customs and habits, the modes of thought, speech, or worship, which have been accepted as traditional, have been the first to feel the effects of the dissolving influences of the time.

I wish to mention specially five of these forces of dissolution :—

1. *The spread of elementary education* has created a new problem, one which the Church has never yet had to face, the problem of a whole people capable of reading, but incapable of estimating the value of what they read. The faculty of reading is in the possession of all ; like other faculties, it demands satisfaction, and to meet its demands there is a ceaseless supply of every sort of literature, ventilating every sort of opinion. The supply is so persistent, rapid, and varied, that it rather destroys than helps the power of thought. Our opinions, however sacred they may be to us, only enter this motley crowd, in which the reading public find occupation and entertainment, and must take their chance with the rest.

2. *The scientific spirit.*—Its influence as a dis-solving force is often exaggerated ; certainly it is not nearly so strong as it was fifty years ago. Science has become more content to work within its own limits, and more humble in its attitude towards regions which lie beyond. It is more deeply conscious of mystery, within, and still more around, the facts which it investigates ; it is there-

fore more reverent in tone. But among educated men this very sense of mystery leads them to question all positive statements, and to shrink from all definite doctrines. Among the uneducated, scraps of scientific thought and speech have a wide currency and seem to contradict the teaching of religion. It is not the thoughts of the really great men of science which reach the populace, but rather the noisy and confident opinions of those camp followers of science who take possession of and trade with the refuse which the main army has long since left behind.

3. *The spirit of Biblical criticism.*—Hitherto the average Englishman's belief in the Bible has not been seriously shaken. Whether or no he followed its precepts, he regarded it as the one and only authority for the Christian religion. As such, he conceived that every detail in it must be equally true; that the whole of the Christian religion was somehow involved in its literal accuracy. Now he finds that dates, authorship, recorded events are uncertain, and this uncertainty affects his whole belief in the Christian revelation. We have only to realize the customary beliefs of the ordinary man, even of the English Churchman, about the Bible to realize also how defenceless he is against the first touch of dissolving criticism. Yet in newspaper and magazine, in the talk of the smoking-room and of the workshop, the spirit

of criticism is ceaselessly at work challenging facts and insinuating doubts. Most men have neither the time nor the capacity to think out these doubts; but an atmosphere of unrest and suspicion is spread around the Faith to which they have been accustomed. You may take it for granted, even of many of the men who still attend Church, that their minds are often a shifting rubble of half-formed doubts and vague uncertainties in which no religious impression or influence can take root and become strong faith and clear conviction. In the case of those who stand aloof from the Church, or fall away, if you track the cause back to its first source, you will find again and again that it was some Biblical difficulty. Trivial enough in itself, like some germ of disease it entered the mind; it found there no counteracting power of thought and knowledge, and slowly it spread its taint around the inner life. Every difficulty, once it comes to the surface in expression, can be met and dealt with, but when it is suppressed it works a havoc quite out of proportion to its own importance. At other times doubt has been open, confident, even violent; in our own day it is rather vague, diffused, and therefore doubly dangerous.

4. *The spirit of independence*—This is a spirit obviously widespread and far-reaching. In the sphere of religion it acts as a kind of resentment

against any teaching which asserts the claim of authority. It is partly due to the all-pervading spirit of competition; every opinion, like every business, must now stand upon its own merits and make its own way. It is partly due to the fault of the clergy in teaching the truth in methods or language often unreal to themselves, or unreal to the men to whom they speak, and then claiming that the statements thus made must be accepted without question. But chiefly it is due to our unhappy divisions; the ceaseless wrangling between Roman Catholic and Anglican, between Church and Dissent, or worse still between the different sections of our own Church, has led to the belief that no religious truth has any real authority at all. God alone knows—we shall perhaps know in the Day of Judgment—the damage which has been done to the credit of Christianity by inter-Christian controversy. Outside the limits of ecclesiastical circles it has created in the mind of the average man an infinite weariness and disgust. That dislike of dogmatism which is so natural to the Englishman seems to be amply justified. He turns with relief to a plain moral teaching which he can understand, or to a vague undenominational religion which seems to provide an escape from denominational discord.

5. This spirit of impatience with the doctrines and institutions of religion accords with another

feature of the times which is of great importance. I shall call attention to it frequently in these lectures. Let me describe it in the words of the Bishop of Southwark as "*a weakening of embodied and a strengthening of diffused Christianity.*" He means that the power of Christianity as embodied in a Creed or a Church, once as in the Middle Ages or at the Reformation the only conceivable form of Christianity, is declining; and the power of Christianity as a sentiment, an ideal diffused through many streams of feeling or action, is increasing. The spirit of Christianity—its moral beauty; its interpretation of the pathos of life; its philanthropy; its enthusiasm for the weak, the suffering, the oppressed; its brotherliness—seems to present itself to men in movements literary, social, political, and religious, which stand quite apart from definite and dogmatic religion. Thus men are able as perhaps never before to satisfy themselves that they can preserve the Christian spirit, without paying any deference to the Christian Creed or the Christian Church.

There are of course other dissolving forces which are equally strong—such as the facilities of travel, the haste to make money, the elaborate organization of amusement—but of these I do not speak. They are all contributory causes to the general restlessness of which I have already spoken. Certainly the outward signs of the dissolution of custom in religion are clear enough. Take only one, in our English life one most significant—the increasing neglect of any religious observance of Sunday. Let us restrict the matter within the limits of our own observation. Follow the career of your own friends who leave the Universities; they are not under the influence of active or resolute doubt, they have no antagonism to Christianity; most of them will keep honourably free from any serious immorality; they will become healthy-minded, hard-working, good-living men; many of them have a real religious sentiment of their own; but in five or ten years how many of them will you find professing any open adherence to Christianity as a definite creed or associating themselves with public worship as professed members of a Church?

This, then, is the atmosphere of questioning, of restlessness, of instability, into which you have to carry your faith and your commission. From one point of view we rightly speak of this dissolution of customary religion as an evil. The force of habit is not to be despised. It is in itself alike a witness and a restraint; it reminds men of religion, it keeps them within the sphere of its influence, it surrounds their daily life with some token of things unseen. We may remember Thomas Carlyle's emphatic words, "our whole

being is an infinite abyss over-arched by habit as
by a thin 'Earth-rind,' laboriously built together.
Without such 'Earth-rind' of habit, call it system
of habits, in a word, fixed ways of acting and
believing—society would not exist at all. Let but
by ill chance your thin 'Earth-rind' be once
broken! The fountains of the great deep boil
forth; fire-fountains, enveloping, engulfing.
Your 'Earth-rind' is shattered, swallowed up;
instead of a grand flowery world there is a waste,
wild, weltering chaos, which has again, with
tumult and struggle, to make itself into a world."

In the light of Carlyle's lurid imagination, this
breaking up of what is customary and habitual
seems black enough, but in the light of Christian
hope and Christian faith—the faith that the ways
of man are under the ordering of God—it is not
simply an evil to be deplored, but an opportunity
to be bought up. There are energies in the very
forces which cause the evil, which can be converted
into powers of recovery. After all, the breach
with custom is often a vague impulse of sincerity.
So far, it has a soul of goodness in it. Honest
revolt is better than dishonest conformity; the
former has at least the element of truth, the latter
has the element of a lie; and a lie is the only
thing in the world that is finally bad. The impulse of sincerity, in so far as it is true, however
vague it may be, cannot rest finally in the con-

fusion and uncertainty of mind to which at first it
leads. Man cannot remain content with chaos.
Order is life's first law, and life is always restless
until it is realized. The instincts, the importuni-
ties, of the human spirit will refuse to remain in
the region of uncertainty ; they will press on to
find truth and conviction. Throw a man back
upon himself, deprived of the foothold of customary
religion, and he will grope for some other basis
upon which he can stand. We see this groping
on every side. The special characteristic of our
literature has been described as a craving for
spiritual rest. Science, abandoning its confident
negations, is finding its way back to God by the
long but sure paths of reverence and wonder.
There is an interest in religion, keen and all-pervading, disclosed in fiction, in the press, in the
daily conversation even of those who profess no
definite form of it.

"Nothing, I believe," said Dr. Westcott,[1] "is
more unjust than to call the spirit of modern
English thought irreligious. On the contrary,
even in its scepticism it clings to religion. There
never was a time when men have had a keener
sense of what religion ought to be and to do.
There never was a time when the demands upon
religion were greater."

Above all, there never has been a time when,

[1] "Words of Faith and Hope," p. 46.

with such pathetic consent, often in such strange voices, the Jesus of the Gospels has been more widely accepted as the Light and Master of human life. Thus even in this apparently restless and unstable generation there seems to be a stir of something coming. The voices are confused and discordant, the steps uncertain and stumbling, there is no clear note of leadership. Yet there is movement, there is life; and where there is life there is always hope. This is our opportunity. We know the only goal which can give final rest and strength to the human spirit; we know that the Christ in man leads him in many ways and in divers fashions to find the Christ in God as the supreme truth and end of life. These dissolving forces which we have considered may become a new opportunity to be bought up by those who understand what the Will of the Lord is.

Let us take each of them in turn, and indicate the spirit in which we can hopefully approach them, and in which we can try to convert them into good.

c

CHAPTER III

1. THE spread of elementary education is a real good; in spite of all appearances, let us have the courage of this faith. It becomes an evil only if it is ill directed and ill used. It is for us to liberate the power of good that is in it from the power of evil, to see that with the gift of reading is given to the people some knowledge of the things that it is worth while to read; to make the elementary schools real nurseries of intelligence and character; to enlist the *mind* of every child in the Sunday-school on the side of religion; to keep in touch with the growing and expanding mind of the boys and girls after they have left school, in reading circle, in Bible-class, in lecture, and in continuation schools; patiently and persistently to respect the intelligence of our people, to believe in it even when there seems to be no response to our belief, to seek for it and prize it when it is found, to give them in language however simple the best thoughts that our own best reading gives to ourselves.

This is the opportunity, this ought to be the ambition, of every true parish priest. The opportunity is one which in a very special sense is presented to us now by recent legislation. The clergy have been partially freed from the burden of the financial maintenance of their schools; future legislation will probably remove the burden still more completely from their shoulders. We may lament the loss of personal influence and control in our schools; but in one sense we can turn the loss into gain. When we were left to find the money to realize our genuine ideals and desires, it was difficult to devote ourselves wholeheartedly to the cause of true educational progress. This difficulty is now greatly lessened. Whatever changes legislation in the near future may bring about in regard to voluntary elementary schools, let no counsels of despair persuade us that the educational work of the Church, and especially of the clergy, is over. These schools are only a means to an end—not an end in themselves. The end which they served—the teaching of definite religious faith and the maintenance in all education of a true religious spirit—remains. If the change of circumstances deprive us of one means, we must make use of others. There is, I am persuaded, a field of enormous opportunity open to the Church of England in bringing a spirit of real care for the children themselves into the management of the public elementary schools and in encouraging the best ideals of their teachers; in promoting and organizing efforts to continue and widen the education of boys and girls when their schooldays are over, and to keep it in touch with religion. If we have courage and patience to make use of this wider opportunity, we shall find that there is still a place for the clergy in the world of education, which will become theirs not so much by virtue of the official position which they hold as by virtue of the knowledge and sympathy which they show.[1]

2. How are we to turn the spread of the scientific spirit into an opportunity to be used for God? The truest answer to this question, so far as it can be given in a few general words, is perhaps this: not certainly by opposing it, not even by attempts to reconcile its conclusions with those of religion, for however excellent such attempts may be in intention, few of us have the scientific knowledge necessary to make them really adequate; but rather indirectly by deepening the sense of mystery of which science is itself increasingly conscious, and then by pleading that life to be lived, no less than Nature to be understood, requires assumptions which must be accepted but cannot be proved. Science within its own limits finds God in Nature, religion rather finds Nature in God. Each supple-

[1] See Appendix B.

ments and helps the other; each has its rightful place in the unity of Truth. Here I may quote the words of one of our most eminent men of science spoken to me the other day: "Science and religion must, after all, be one in the mind of God, and if each is true to its own sphere, in His own time He will make them one in the mind of man." Meanwhile, what is essential is, that the man of religion and the man of science should understand and sympathize with the methods which each follows, and with the spirit by which each is inspired.[1]

3. How are we to meet the sense of uncertainty caused by the advances of Biblical criticism? Here, for the answer we need, some of us at least can turn to our own experience. We feel that for ourselves we have got beyond the elementary difficulties which seem so seriously to distress our brothers, both educated and uneducated. We can see, for example, the incomparable dignity and truth of the first chapters of Genesis without supposing that they are an exact anticipation of the results of scientific research. We can discern the place which the rude ethics of rough ages providentially had in God's patient training of Israel, and through Israel of mankind. We can see that questions as to date or authorship do not

[1] I may refer the reader to the very suggestive addresses by the Rev. P. N. Waggett, entitled "The Scientific Temper in Religion," published by Messrs. Longmans, Green, and Co.

really affect the value of the message or witness of
the books of the Bible. We have learnt to recognize and welcome the human element in them, and
have found that it deepens instead of destroying
our faith in the element which is divine. Let us
ask how it is that we have been able to reach this
position. Is it not because we have learnt to study
the Bible as a whole, to distinguish the temporal
from the eternal in a progressive revelation, to
study what inspiration is in the light, not of
theories about it, but of the Bible itself, to consider the Bible in its true relation to Christ, the
centre of its message, and to the history of the
Christian Church, its special and appointed
witness? But many even of the more thoughtful
men whom we shall meet in our visits, or to whom
we shall speak in our churches, are still ignorant
of that method of conceiving and studying the
Bible which has done so much for us in enriching and strengthening our faith in its claims.
They still believe, even those who have read some
critical literature, that the Christian faith is itself
bound up with a conception of the Bible which
we ourselves have passed beyond, a conception
which they naturally enough feel to be incapable
of meeting the challenge of facts. We have,
then, simply to teach our people as we ourselves
have been taught how to read the Bible. It is not
our business—certainly not in our public teaching

—to argue vexed points of scholarship, or to obtrude the latest fancies of the critical imagination. We have simply to teach that positive revelation of which the Bible is a record, in language which brings no trace of the disputes of the schools. We have to teach men to know with a real human sympathy the lives, the history, the characters of the Bible writers. We have in our public instructions to show people how to study the books of the Bible as a whole. Thus we shall communicate the standpoint which we ourselves have reached, and then insensibly, without even being aware perhaps of any violent change in their ordinary conception, they will find themselves standing above and beyond the difficulties which puzzled them. When we consider the place which the Providence of God has assigned to the Bible in our English Church, and the peril to which that place is now exposed, there is a special and imperative summons addressed to us to undertake the duty of its defence. Our ambition should be to restore their Bible to Englishmen, and to restore it enriched and quickened by a truer knowledge and a wiser faith.[1]

4. How are we to meet the spirit of independence, of the dislike of authority? Doubtless it

[1] On this subject I would refer the reader to a collection of his addresses and sermons "On Holy Scripture and Criticism," by Dr. Ryle, the Bishop of Winchester, particularly to chapters ii. and iii.

seems to us an evil, perhaps the characteristic evil of the English temperament; but let us beware, as I shall have to insist repeatedly in these lectures, of the bias of our own professional position as clergy of the English Church. We are only too readily inclined to dislike and even resent any questioning of our assertions. Let us rather meet this spirit of independence with a certain sympathy; it is, after all, at the worst the defect of an English virtue—the love of freedom. The English Church is the Church primarily of English people; its great aim should be to train its children, not to mere unquestioning obedience, but rather to an obedience which is intelligent and free. Let me quote the words of Bishop Creighton :[1] "Steadfast in its hold on the faith and on the sacraments by its unbroken link with the past, (our Church) exists for the maintenence of God's truth, and its application to the needs of man, not for the purpose of upholding its own power. A Church fitted for free men, training them in knowledge and reverence alike; disentangling the spirit from the form, because of its close contact with sons who love their mother, and frankly speak out their minds."

Our best chance of removing what is false in the spirit of independence is to respect what is true. To be practical, let us in our teaching, and

[1] "Church and Nation," p. 214.

above all in our visiting, instead of avoiding as
an awkward and difficult person, rather seek out
and pay special attention to, the man of intelligent
mind and speech, even if his questions are awkward and his criticisms caustic. Do not let us
spend all our time in perfecting the docility of the
docile ; let us give some of it to winning the
freedom of the free. In thus meeting the spirit of
independence we are not to create any suspicion
that we doubt the authority of our own message,
nor in any way to belittle it or apologize for it.
We have simply to remember the abiding lesson
of the pregnant words, "He taught as one having
authority, and not as the Scribes." The authority
which commends itself and does not arouse resentment, is that which clear single-minded hold
upon truth, and simple earnest and non-con-
ventional modes of expressing it, never fail to
exercise. We have to present the truth committed to us in forms which can touch the lives
and thoughts of the actual men and women we
know, with the simplicity of direct conviction ; we
have to clothe it in words which can convey a real
meaning to the actual men and women to whom
we speak. Too often Church doctrine is repeated
by the clergy as if it were a lesson learned by
rote, as if it were a system in the air without any
context and background in actual human experience and need.

"Recollect," wrote Dr. Pusey,[1] "that you have not been called into the vineyard to preach a system, much less the externals of a system, but to tend your Master's sheep and lambs, to feed them and guard them as one who will have to give account."

Above all we have to teach positive truth without always denying or criticizing developments of it with which we do not agree. We have to teach, as it were, with a straight eye upon the souls and minds of our own people, not with a side eye upon what we consider the errors of other teachers. The Bishop of Birmingham, in explaining how parties in the English Church have taken their rise as reactions against exaggerations of truth, made an appeal which I would cordially re-echo: "Brothers, do not let us be always living in reactions." The English Church claims to have returned to the primitive and uncontroversial age of theology; let us betake ourselves in our own reading and teaching to that source, and steep our minds in the spirit of the New Testament and of the primitive Church. Let the doctrines of the Church come to our own minds in the shapes which they had before they were twisted by the troubles of the Middle Ages or of the Reformation; let us teach them faithfully and patiently in simple, untechnical language which ordinary

[1] "Life," II, 145.

people can understand ; then let us leave them to work their own way in the mind and conscience. If we could have for a single generation a truce of God even within the limits of our own English Church, based upon the acceptance of the New Testament and the teaching of the early undivided Church, I do not believe that we should ever return to the miserable warfare upon which we waste so much of our energies and lose so much of our charity. There are not wanting hopeful signs of the possibilities of such a truce.[1] Let it be one of our ambitions to promote, first its coming, and then its staying.

5. Lastly, consider that dissolving force which I described in the words of the Bishop of Southwark as "the weakening of embodied, and the strengthening of diffused Christianity." To us, pledged as we are to the great and steadying tradition of the creed and discipline of the historic Church, this force must seem to be in many ways an evil. Where we meet with it in its negative aspect, as what is called undenominationalism, or even in its positive aspect, as a strong sentiment of philanthropy, it discloses dangerous tendencies.

---

[1] These lectures were delivered before the Dean of Canterbury and his friends had formulated and submitted to the Archbishop of Canterbury their "Appeal to the First Six Centuries." So long as such an appeal is treated as the expression of a spirit or ideal, and not turned (so to say) into a new Act of Uniformity, it must surely commend itself to all peaceable sons of the Church.

I cannot do better than use the words of the Bishop of Southwark: "Evidently what is diffusively Christian by its very nature shades off and grades down into what is not Christian at all. Short of this, it is often capricious, shallow, and unbalanced in its forms; much of its teaching is washy and thin; it is apt to follow the line of least resistance in dealing with human wilfulness and laxity; it has little power to control if it does not even flatter individual self-assertion; it knows little of the mighty strength of spiritual discipline; it can wield very imperfectly the forces of loyalty and corporate conviction."[1]

We are convinced that among the special needs of our own day and generation are just the spirit which a firm creed, and the concentration and enthusiasm which the life of a definite body, alone can give. But here again in this very tendency, in spite of its evil side, we can discern a truth and worth from which we have much to learn, and which we must seek to lead on to their highest realization in the Christ Whom we believe. In the first place, it is foolish to insist always upon the logical weakness of what is called "our common Christianity," and to be perpetually, in season and out of season, insisting upon its inadequacy. We ought rather to recognize with gratitude and hope

[1] "The Church's Failure and the Work of Christ," p. 10. The charge delivered to the Diocese of Rochester when Dr. Talbot was Bishop of that diocese.

that there is so much of the Christian faith which
is common to all who "profess and call themselves Christians." We ought never, after a
fashion far too prevalent, to sneer at "our common
Christianity" as if it were something scarcely worth
having, but rather to prize it, as at least the token
and earnest of a unity deeper than our divisions.
But, beyond this, in the diffusive Christian spirit
or sentiment may we not see something nobler
and truer than a mere revolt against Church
creeds and institutions? It may well be that the
Spirit of Christ, straitened by the sloth and
timorousness of His Church, by its failure to
respond to the whole width of His message,
passes beyond its limits and reaches and touches
men and movements outside its fold. We ought
not grudgingly to acknowledge but thankfully to
welcome these signs that the Spirit of God is in
many ways doing a work outside His Church,
which His Church itself is incapable of doing.
Yet it is a work from which His Church may gain ;
for after all this "diffused" Spirit of Christianity is
preparing a moral soil into which the Church may
go forth with its clearer, surer faith, to sow its own
seed, and to reap its own harvest. We must learn
to recognize and to welcome the footprints of
Christ even when we see them far outside the
highway of His Church.

In the second place, this diffusive Christianity

may serve to recall to the mind and teaching of the
Church a truth as to Christ's Person and office in
their relation to Man, which it has sometimes been
slow to realize and present to the world. It is the
truth that He is not only One who saves us from
our sins, but One who vindicates and completes
all that is true and noble in human life and
thought. In our own minds by thought, study,
and imagination, we must widen and deepen our
hold upon the faith of the Incarnation, so as to be
ready to see Christ in all spheres of true human
life, to open the eyes of men to discern His Presence there, and thus to draw them through their
own best human experience to understand and welcome His claim. I do not hesitate to quote again
from Bishop Talbot's charge to the Diocese of
Rochester, for I am anxious that all who hear
or read these lectures should study the weighty
words, and catch something of the spirit of that
striking and suggestive address.[1] "I pray you,"
he says, "to recognize that these two truths of
fulfilment in Christ, and of what I called the
diffusive force, combine with and complement one
another. For taken together they mean, so to
speak, that the lines run inward from all life into
Him, and outward from Him into all life. I would
urge you with passionate earnestness so to study
Christ in this double context with the life of the

[1] "The Church's Failure and the Work of Christ," cf. p. 18.

race in which He was incarnate, and so to present Him to men."

Lastly, we must seek by God's grace to make our own Christian character—the character which claims to be based upon the Creed, and to be disciplined by the Church, the character which men watch in ourselves and in our Church people —to make this character a reflection in the circumstances of modern life of what the Incarnation was meant to be to mankind. The Church Christian ought to be the man who embodies all that is best and most attractive in this diffused Christianity, the man who by the instinct of life realizes and expresses what these wider movements often painfully and even artificially strive after, namely, sympathy with all true human activities, charity, brotherliness, eagerness for social service. It is at all times, and in all places, certain that the Christian life is the truest and most cogent apology for the Christian Faith. This after all is the Bible which all men read, and of whose inspiration no man can doubt. If the Church in our different parishes were a society of men and women who were not only faithful to the traditions of their own community but were also foremost in all common effort for the enriching and uplifting of human life, then surely good men everywhere would be not repelled by its narrowness, but attracted by its sympathy. Then we

should have some chance of proving in fact
what we believe in theory, that the Church is
the divinely appointed organ through which, not
exclusively but most directly, the Spirit of God
purifies, redeems, and consecrates humanity. Let
us then go forth to our great work inspired by the
hope of winning in some small corner of the great
campaign that noblest Christian victory, by which
the forces that are against us are not merely
resisted, but brought over to our own side.

CHAPTER IV

WE pass now to the second characteristic evil of the time, of which I specially wish to speak. The first was the dissolution of definite faith and of the customs and institutions of religion; the second is the existence in our midst of a vast class in which there is no definite faith and no customary religion to dissolve—a class which, as a class, stands outside the Christian Church, its creed, its observances, and its institutions. I mean, of course, the great working class gathered with increasing density in our cities and large towns. When I speak in this context of the Church, I include all religious bodies; and when I speak of the working class, I am not thinking of individuals within it, who in the aggregate form, thank God, a large number of devout Christians, but of the working class as a whole. It is impossible to resist the conclusion of Mr. Charles Booth, that it "stands outside any organized religious body." This conclusion has been of late brought home to us, so far as London is concerned, with special force by the investigations of Mr. Booth and of his colleagues, and by the religious census which was undertaken by the "Daily News." I do not think that London in this respect stands worse than other great towns. It is obvious—indeed, it was inevitable—that both the book and the census made mistakes in details, sometimes serious enough. It is obvious, as we shall see later, that no inquiry undertaken at a definite time and necessarily dealing with outward evidence can rightly estimate tendencies and movements which are as real as, and often far more important than, statistical facts. Statistics, as the very word implies, deal with things as they stand, as they are at some moment arbitrarily selected : true history deals with things as they were, and as they are coming to be. But as giving a broad statement of the existing situation, the main conclusion of these inquiries cannot be seriously challenged.[1] It is a conclusion which is not new to those whose work has lain in our great cities and towns. The Bishop of London, for example, found as the result of his inquiries in certain large centres of labour, that only one per cent. of the workmen admitted that they belonged to any Christian body. It is a conclusion confirmed by my own experience. If you attend a gathering of working men in the East End of London on some political

[1] Cf. Appendix C.

or social question, you can discern at a glance that they are a different sort of men altogether from those whom you meet in church or chapel.

It is the mere truth, that the mass of our people are, except for a few vague sentiments and the traditional observance of certain Christian ceremonies, the real meaning of which they scarcely understand—such as baptism, churching, or marriage—wholly outside the pale of definite and organized Christianity. Now we do well to describe this fact as a portentous evil. The want of any real and effective place for religion in the lives and habits of the great majority of our fellow-countrymen is a mighty hindrance to the advancement of the Kingdom of God. It is scarcely possible for us to estimate the effect upon our own lives of the inherited traditions and associations of religion. They have formed a temperament, a disposition, a set of instincts, which are really the basis of our religious life. How can we estimate what we owe to the early prayers which we were taught under the most hallowed influences, to the gradual moulding of the habits and thoughts of our child-life, to the school chapel, to the memories of Confirmation, or to the example of parents? All these have formed an influence not less strong because we are scarcely conscious of it; they constitute a sort of second nature, which survives all changes. Even when men have yielded to some of the dissolving forces of which I have spoken, as I know by experience, these embedded associations and instincts of the Christian religion remain constant in the background of life. But when you visit from house to house in some dingy city street, never forget, either that you owe more than you can tell to your traditional background of religion, or that most of those whom you meet have never had it.

Nay, must we not admit that all the conditions of their life have been unfavourable to the development of religion? Think of the constituents of your own experience which have made steadily for religion. There was the home; but how can home be a centre of hallowed influences to numbers of even decent and hard-working folk, who are obliged to live huddled like sheep in a pen, without any possibilities of privacy or quiet? We probably owe more than we know to the influences of Nature; but what uplifting power can there be in the environment of acres of dull drick and long lines of mean streets? As one of our Bishops recently asked: "What would you know of the stars if you had never seen them out of London?" Try to consider the influence upon your own lives of the example or of the friendship of high and noble characters, and remember that masses of our people have never come into contact, much less friendship, with any man or woman of real refinement of character, or seen among their acquaintances the strength and sweetness of religion. Once again, the work in which most of us have been, or are, engaged, has been of itself an influence capable of disciplining or even of raising our character. There is, indeed, a true and real nobility of toil; but it is hard to realize it in the narrow and cramping employments in which, owing to the elaborate division of labour, most of our people spend eight hours at least for six days in the week. What would our life be if our life-work were to make the legs of a chair or the heels of a boot, or to fill match-boxes, or to stick the labels upon them? This is a type of labour which, so far from quickening, deadens the faculties of mind, and creates a natural craving for the relief of excitement, or for the mere blank of physical rest from toil. The working man's Sunday is after all the natural effect of causes left to work themselves out unchecked upon his body and mind. Heredity, environment, occupation, the most enduring because the most unconscious influences of life, are, among multitudes of our working folk, against any religion which makes demands upon thought or effort. It is not opposition which you will encounter, but blank indifference—an indifference often the more perplexing because it is wholly good-natured. I cannot better summarize the difficulty than in the words of a working man in East London : " It isn't that we have anything against your religion ; the whole thing doesn't touch us any closer than the moon."

This, then, is an evil the burden of which we have to lay upon our souls. It is a false optimism which ever tries to forget it. To us as Church-men it is nothing but the grimmest and most melancholy consolation that other religious bodies are as little in touch as we are with this mass of people. In the midst of all your eager and mani-fold tending of the sheep who are in the fold, never shut out the thought of the far larger num-ber who are still wandering in the wilderness. Those of us who are called to labour in our great towns have special need of remembering the words which were solemnly spoken to us at our ordina-tion, that we were "to seek for Christ's sheep that are dispersed abroad, and for His children who are in the midst of this naughty world, that they may be saved through Christ for ever." But here again we must not allow ourselves merely to dwell upon the evil, or allow ourselves to be depressed or paralysed by its extent. In facing it frankly, at least we know what the Will of the Lord is, and must seek even within it for the signs of opportunities to be bought up in a spirit of cour-age, faith, and hope ; and these signs of encour-agement are not wanting.

1. Our cities and great towns are at least an open mission field; the land is yet to be possessed; and there is something of honour and cheer in the command, "Go over and possess it." We are dealing with a people not lost to the Church, but waiting to be won. They have not fallen from the Church, for they were never within it. No phrase could be more misleading than that which is often on men's lips—the lapsed masses. It is true that when we consider the thousands who have passed through our day and Sunday schools into a life of indifference there seems to be some truth in the phrase; but in fact our methods seem to have failed to reach the real life of the child or to keep hold of it when school days are over. These thousands were never really shepherded and brought securely within the fold. It is, indeed, not here among our working folk that we find "the lapsed masses," but rather in the classes who have enjoyed better opportunities, even among those who still attend our churches by force of heredity or social custom, but acquiesce in an entire lapse of the whole inner meaning of their Christian profession. Our working classes are at least not implicated in an inconsistency which has become habitual; they are, let me repeat, an open mission field in which the Church is called to work with infinite patience, persistence, sympathy, and hope.

2. The ground has been already in many ways prepared for us. Speaking generally, we may say that the missionary effort of the Church in the great towns within the parochial system has been at work for not much more than sixty years. Within that time the devoted labours of thousands of faithful parish priests, now grown grey in their service or passed to their rest, have been preparing the way through difficulties which were greater far than ours, and their courage remains for our example. One great work the influence of their own lives and of the few whom they have gathered around them has already accomplished. It has stemmed the tide of mere savagery; it has to a large extent "overcome the beast" in our great cities; it has at least brought the silent witness of religion into the very midst of the people; it has gradually turned sullen opposition into something like respect for the clergy and their message. As the Bishop of London has truly said, "It is the imaginary, impalpable thing called the Church they object to; their own clergy, if they work, they love." This is the vantage ground which the pioneers of the last sixty years have secured for us : we have only to enter into their labours.

3. Let us never doubt the real capacity for religion in these separated masses. There is (a) the fact of supreme importance, though very often

forgotten, that after all they are made in the
Image of God; they have souls with God-
given instincts, fears, and desires. Most of them
have been baptized; and though separated from
the Church, they are not, and cannot be, separated from the unseen influence of the Spirit of
God, Who breathes where He lists, and from a
Love which is real for each of them with the
intense reality of the Cross. Never forget when
you visit a house that the Spirit of God has been
a visitor before you, preparing the way in a
manner beyond your sight in the inner character
of its people. For (b) there are qualities of
character in our working folk which are beautiful
in themselves and full of promise, such as their
patience, kindliness, neighbourliness and wonderful good cheer. These are qualities often rude
and undisciplined, but nevertheless a foundation
for the most primary virtues of Christianity, a
foundation which I believe our working folk
possess in a larger and fuller degree than can be
found even among the classes who observe a
customary religion. The Samaritan of the street
is often in spirit nearer Christ the Divine neighbour than many a priest or Levite of the Church.
(c) Moreover, you must always remember that
there remains somehow and somewhere in the
working classes a very real sentiment of religion.
It is doubtless vague and ignorant, linked, per-

haps, with fast-fading memories of lessons in the Sunday-school, but not yet crushed out; often in time of trouble or trial it will emerge with pathetic simplicity and sincerity. They have, as a rule, belief in a Supreme Being. Their conception of God is, indeed, coloured by their own imperfect standard of conscience; it tends to become the conception of a Being of unlimited good nature,[1] a conception which, if we think of it, however perverted it may be, has a pathos of its own when we remember the conditions of the world with which they are surrounded. It is a belief indefinite, because their natural poverty of imagination makes it intensely difficult for them to realise things unseen. Yet it is a belief which is capable of being trained and deepened. There is also—how shall I describe it?—a very real feeling for Christ. His Name, however often by force of custom it is taken in vain in daily speech, still carries with it at special moments a suggestion of infinite tenderness and sympathy for the poor and toiling, for those that "labour and are heavy-laden." This feeling witnesses to the deep human yearning for some Heart of Compassion behind the sad and perplexing shows of

[1] I hope that the insertion here may be pardoned of the remark of an East Ender after listening to a religious address, for the point of it is that there was not the slightest intention of irreverence—"Well, I always did believe meself that Gawd was a kind gentleman."

things. I believe that it has been wonderfully
preserved among our people by the popular
hymns which most of them still know and which
remain as a legacy of influence from that first
great missionary enterprise of the Wesleys and
their friends. At present at least this sentiment
of religion is too deep and general to be overcome by the arguments and sneers of infidel
lecturers, or newspapers, or workshop talk. Let
me give one simple illustration. I was once
having a discussion with a large crowd of working men, many of them "free-thinking" Socialists.
A speaker had been arguing that Christ was a
mere man; he made his points well, and they
were greeted with applause. My reply was
simply the familiar story of Charles Lamb's inter-
ruption of a conversation about the great men of
the past: "I will tell you what it is. If Shake-
speare were to enter this room, we should all
stand; but if Christ were to enter, we should all
kneel." I shall never forget the deep hush of
instinctive assent which came over the audience
as they heard these words. It seemed as if the
Spirit of Christ had indeed entered. The momen-
tary silence was broken by a man sitting beneath
me, who muttered aloud, "Yes; after all, that's
true."

4. There is a great encouragement for us in
the type of Christian life which those who are

gathered in from this outside world readily disclose. It is a type sincere, simple, brotherly.

(*a*) Its sincerity is secured in almost all great towns by the rude but sure test of opposition and persecution. I know it to be true from experience in Leeds, Portsmouth, and East London, that almost every man or woman, boy or girl, who has the courage to profess the desire to live a Christian life, or even to acknowledge membership in some Christian body, must count the cost; and the cost is paid in the endurance of taunts, and scoffs and gibes, even sometimes of real loss of money or advancement in work. So long as people merely attend casual Pleasant Sunday Afternoons, or Watch Night services, or sensationally advertised undenominational missions, or the addresses, let us say, of "boy preachers" or other exciting evangelists, they pass unnoticed; but as soon as they make a distinct stand as Christians against accepted customs of talk or social life, or have the courage to come out on the side of Christianity by open and loyal membership of Church or Chapel; above all, as soon as they make such a definite and open choice of religion as Confirmation, then in some form the world still exacts the penalty of a Cross.

It is this fact which always gives a unique sense of reality at once pathetic and inspiring to a Confirmation in the East End of London. I can think of a poor woman who, because her Confirmation was to be the sealing of her resolve to give up drink, was, on its eve, tied to a chair while her husband and two of his mates tried to force brandy down her throat : of a lad who came late to the Confirmation, obviously bruised and distressed, because he had fought his way to church through the street-gang to whom he had once belonged : of a factory-girl of whose hard struggles against temptation I had known, passing me as I met the candidates going to their places and saying, "Oh, Bishop, pray for me : I'm afraid of myself": of a man, who, for a whole week after his Confirmation, had to endure, in silence, at the dinner hour in his workshop, a mock-repetition of the ceremony conducted by his fellow-workmen. But, indeed, there is scarcely any East End Confirmation held at which I do not hear of some such tale of courage and endurance ; and almost every parish priest could tell many similar tales from his own experience. There are times when one almost welcomes the absence of the helps of custom and tradition, since it leads to a religion which depends upon choice, and upon a choice which is indeed signed with the Sign of the Cross.

(*b*) In the second place, the type of Christianity which discloses itself among our working folk is one which accepts, with all simplicity, an exacting moral standard. It is here that the customary Christianity of other classes is so lamentably weak. The ordinary habits of their world have attained a certain respectability; but, on the other hand, the habits of the Christian have largely accommodated themselves to the conventions of the world. Is it an exaggeration to say that the Christianity of the average professing Churchman in the upper and middle classes stands for very little definite moral witness? But among the classes whose social conventions involve, let us say, swearing, drinking, looseness of talk, there the mere profession of Christianity, still more the allegiance to some Christian body, separates a man from his fellows, by putting a mark of moral singularity upon him. "The hardest thing about it," said a man to me the other day of his new Christian life, "is that it means breaking with my old pals." The moral standard may be in itself still rude, defective, untrained, but at least there is in it the saving salt of struggle. To us, with our upbringing, opportunities, ideals, it may often seem disappointing; but never forget that even the mere moral respectability with which we are apt sometimes to be impatient may mean a moral effort far greater than any we have ever been called upon to make. We clergy may well be humble if we realize at what moral cost many a working man merely sits before us in church.

You may sometimes sigh for the stimulus of a crowded church, but there may be more power of moral effort, more strength of moral witness, in the little band of faithful people scattered up and down the nave, than in many a thronged congregation of customary Christians.

(c) In the third place, the type of Christianity which discloses itself among our working folk is instinctively social and brotherly. Give to a congregation of well-dressed people your message that their Church is meant to be a society, a brotherhood, a comradeship of faith, of worship, and of work, and you feel that you are speaking to deaf ears ; but give that message to a congregation of working-class people and all that is best in them rises in response to it.

CHAPTER V

THESE then are our encouragements; and they point to the lines of opportunity which we have to use in the name of the Lord and Brother of men. They must have been very feebly described if they do not of themselves at once suggest the method and spirit in which we are called upon to work among our great town populations. But let us ask more particularly in what ways we are to buy up opportunity thus presented to us.

1. We must go about our work in a spirit of the broadest human sympathy. Before we attempt to impress our points of view about religion upon the people, we must try to discover and appreciate theirs. We must put ourselves in their position, so wholly different from our own, and this means a real effort of sustained sympathy. We continually make the mistake of applying our own ideal of religion or worship, without first studying the human material which we have to mould. It is as if the painter were to set to work without understanding his colours, or the sculptor

without understanding the qualities of his clay. Thus in visiting our first object should be, not to talk, in a manner however edifying, but rather to listen, to draw out the man or woman before us as they are. Every person whom we thus learn to understand becomes an interpreter of his or her class to us. We learn from them the words that are used in their own circle, and the real meaning which they carry; we learn the characteristic ways in which the people think. We must always keep the Priest in us yoked to the man ; our priestly ideal will prevent us from attempting too little, our human sympathy will prevent us from expecting too much. Moreover, this pastoral sympathy ought always to have a dash of humour in it, of that true humour which is always near of kin to tears. Never let these inner springs of humour be dried up, for this is one of the most frequent causes of pastoral failure. The soldiers, sailors, costermongers, and dockyard labourers of Portsmouth followed "Father Dolling" because they lived and laughed with "Brother Bob." Believe me, love, deep, real, and human, comes often to us along the way of laughter. While the Priest within us knows "no man after the flesh," that is, sees in every man the immortal soul for which Christ died and for which His love yearns, the man within us likes the poor, perverse, perplexing flesh, and by liking lifts. The Priest within us

E

keeps us persistent, the man within us keeps us patient ; this blending of persistence and patience is the ideal of the *Pastor in parochia*.

2. This human sympathy will lead us to adapt our work and witness to the capacities of our people. Let us remember from the first, and never forget, that if we are to be understood by ordinary working folk in our talks with them and in our sermons we must get rid of two-thirds of our ordinary vocabulary. It is scarcely too much to say that it is as necessary to begin your ministry in Leeds or East London by learning the language of the people, as it would be in Africa or China ; otherwise all your eloquence will be mere talking in the air. So far as Church services are concerned, remember that the working man and working woman of to-day cannot be expected all at once to find in the language of Elizabethan literature, which we so fervently admire in the Prayer Book, the language of their own hearts. Until it is interpreted, it is to a large extent a foreign language. As we shall see more fully in the last lecture, we must in special services in church and mission hall, in talks by the fireside, and in prayers by the bedside, reach the people by words which touch real heart-chords within them.

3. Though sympathetic in spirit and elastic in method, we must be rigorous in maintaining a high standard of what the Christian profession

morally means. Let us be infinitely patient and considerate in bringing our people up to the level of the Christian life; but we must never try to make the process short and easy by bringing the Christian life down to the level of the people. Let nothing tempt us to bridge the chasm between the people and the Church by belittling the claims of Christ. They know, as we have seen, that it is hard to be a Christian; we must beware of making it too easy. We must keep religion in touch with their own best conscience. We are simply throwing away our opportunity if in any way we try to lower their own standard of what a Christian ought to be. Better, far, to wait for years till a man finds his own way by hard struggle to Christ and His Church, than to let him suppose that it is a simple thing for him to profess and call himself a Christian. The mistakes of the past are a warning in this direction for the future. It is because he loves souls that the pastor will be resolute, in the administration of charity, to protect his people from the taint and temptation of religious bribery. It is because he loves souls that he will guard against indiscriminate Baptism; he will rather surround that Sacrament with every circumstance of dignity and solemnity, so that at least in this mission field the poorest shall understand, in a way seldom understood by the richest, what it means to be a Christian. It is because he loves souls that he will never sweep his school-children into Confirmation, or care more for the number than for the earnestness of his candidates. It is love of souls which will prevent him from urging his people to come to the Holy Communion, as if it were a sort of rule with a magic efficacy of its own, without regard to the moral condition in which they are standing. It is because he loves souls that he will try to preserve whatever remnants are left to the English Church of that godly discipline which once a year he solemnly professes his desire to restore. The true pastor will never indeed allow his care of the faithful to make him forget the mass of indifferent people around him ; he will try to know all and be the friend of all ; but he will make it his main object to see that his faithful, however few, are at least consistent Christians. It is only a summary of prolonged experience to say that every consistent member is an addition to the missionary force of the Church, while every inconsistent member is an addition to its stumbling-blocks. The pastor's object is never to make his church full, but to make it a power for Christ ; not to attract numbers, but to train Christians ; as the Bishop of Birmingham shortly puts it : " It is not more, but better Christians, that we want." A tradesman once said to me, " I will deal with your Christian shop when I see that the people it turns out are more *up to sample*." Let us try in this mission field of the towns to make the Church "an honest business."

4. We must present the Church to the people in our great towns in the aspect that is most likely to attract them, by most directly meeting their deepest needs. We shall find that this aspect for which they are waiting is also the aspect of Church life which is the most primitive, which is most full of the freshness of the early springtide of the Church. For the further we go back in its history, the more we recognize that the Church in each place had the marks of a real, rich, brotherly, common life. In the midst of all the sundering tendencies of persecution and of the break-up of the ancient world, Christianity held together by a sort of family instinct. The Church was the home, the household of God, and the members were linked together in a tie of brotherhood. This is precisely the aspect of the Church which will appeal to the mass of the people in our great towns. In the midst of the loneliness of moral witness, the restlessness of great crowds, the weariness of long monotonous labour, all the disintegrating influences of city life, it ought surely to be a relief to them to find in their Church a home, a place of friends, where there is common life, common speech, common worship, and a warm and strengthening spirit of brotherhood.

This is indeed, as I shall try to insist more fully later on, the Church revival to which our Living Head at this time specially calls us. It comes to complete the great revival of the last century. We but feebly pay our debt, our immeasurable debt, to that revival by supposing that it leaves no room for further development. Let me once more quote the words of the Bishop of Southwark:[1] "The Church was thought of more as the authority for guarding revelation, and as the depository of truth and grace, than as the living, many-functioned brotherhood working in the power of the Spirit." It is that conception of the Church which we have now to restore and to realize everywhere, and not least in our great towns.

5. And, last, we must seek to make this body, that is the Church, in every parish a corporate power for the advancement of the Kingdom of God. In regard to the religious work of the parish, our question should be not always, How much can I do? but as often, How much can I get this brotherhood of Christ to do? In social work, that is in removing the stones, the economic stones, which bar the way of those who seek to raise the spirit of the working classes, such as intemperance, insanitary conditions, overcrowding, betting, vulgarity of amusement, irregularity of trade, the Church of England has not taken the

[1] "The Church's Failure and the Work of Christ," p. 38.

lead which she might have taken ; the reason is not because its clergy have not been keen, but because its own public opinion has not been organized. The Church will attract the best sort of working man when it is seen to give to the cause of social reform the moral strength and patience which no other organization, as they know, can give.

So far, then, from being discouraged by this great mass of people not yet brought within the fold of Christ, let us rather see in it the call to realize in their midst a new and higher type of the Christian Church, one truer to the spirit of the New Testament, one which has almost vanished from the Christian life of other classes. It is the inspiration of this ideal which makes one feel that there is no opportunity so hopeful as that which lies before the English Church in the great open mission field of our crowded cities.

CHAPTER VI

WE have now made a review of two of the special difficulties of our time and of the spirit in which we must approach them. By understanding what the will of the Lord is, we are to buy them up as opportunities for Christ and His Church. I have thought it best even at the risk of anticipating much which must be repeated later, to begin by stating our position in general terms ; but it is now necessary to fill in the outline thus indicated with greater detail.

And first, let us attempt to answer the question —For the fulfilment of the task, what manner of men must we ourselves be trying to be? In other words, our subject is our own personal equipment, intellectual and spiritual, for meeting the need and the opportunity presented to us. We shall consider the subject as it specially bears upon the two great problems which have been sketched.

First, *our intellectual equipment*. I. With what intellectual equipment are we to meet the dissolving tendencies of the time? The general answer is simply—we have to know where we ourselves stand, and why. There is at least one welcome and bracing element in the mental atmosphere by which we are surrounded, a craving for reality. This, as we saw, is the aspect of hope and promise in the current reaction against the customs and conventions of religion. But it is only a part of a much wider movement. We cannot doubt that one of the reasons for the attraction, the success, and the influence of scientific inquiry is, that it is felt to be in touch with real facts. The historical method applied with so much care and persistence to the study of philosophy and religion and of all institutions, social, political, and ecclesiastical, witnesses, in spite of much extravagance in its application, to the same desire to get a foothold on foundations of fact. In the sphere of art and literature the method which is loosely expressed by the term "realism" represents, with much that is strained and affected, and even incongruous with the true principles of art, a worthy and disinterested desire to see and present things as they really are. Everywhere the mind of man is pressing beyond the traditional and conventional, to the real and living. It is into this atmosphere that we are to bring our message of faith. The day of contented and unthinking acquiescence in all ranks of society is over. You may remember the comment of Tennyson's "Northern Farmer" on the parson's sermon :

" An' I niver knaw'd whot a meän'd, but I thowt a 'ad summat to
saäy.
An' I thowt a said whot a owt to 'a said, an' so I coom'd awaäy."

That spirit, with its illusive security, is dead. In
the mental atmosphere which we breathe, what is
merely conventional, unreal, impersonal, will
assuredly wither. Now, if ever, we must get rid
of what Charles Kingsley used to call "accursed
secondhandishness." We must be able, if our
words are to secure a hearing, to give an impression of knowledge, at first hand, of ἐπίγνωσις—
knowledge, that is, which comes not so much from
extent of learning as from intensity of grasp.
We cannot indeed hope at once, or ever, to attain
this sort of knowledge over the whole field of
theology, over even that section of the field of
theology which is covered by the doctrines of the
Church, and is specially committed to us. There
must always be, and especially at first, the element of venture in our profession of faith. It
involves an act—in itself, if we think it out, a
reasonable act—of choice rather than of complete
understanding. When the understanding is still
uncertain, the will leads us to take our stand by
the Church and its message; to rely on the
strength and persistence of the historic Christian
experience. Yet from the first and always there
are two marks of reality which we can all possess.

(1) First, we can surely know the point at which,

or through which, the Christian faith primarily reaches and holds our own personal thought and life. To some it may be the great truth of the Fatherhood of God; to some the character and teaching of Jesus; to some the moral mastery which He exercises over them; to some the appeal of the needs of their fellow-men, which they feel they can best meet in His service: but whatever that point of primary influence may be, every man who with any sincerity means to enter, or has entered, the Ministry, ought at least to *know* what it is. It is for him the starting-point of his witness, his own personal way of truth. If he follows it out loyally it will lead him gradually to an ever clearer and more personal hold upon the other contents of the Faith. For, varied as are the ways in which the Faith is realized, it is in itself one and indivisible, an organic unity. We must surely be singularly lacking in the power of reflection upon our own experience, we are certainly ill equipped for our work, unless we are all aware in our own personal life of some such arresting point of truth, some aspect—one or more—which appeals to us with special and constraining force, which we hold because we know that it holds us. This will always be our own real, because personal, contribution to the cause of the Christian faith.

(2) Second, we can all make sure at least of our

own mental attitude towards the questions which specially occupy the mind and trouble the faith of our generation. Of these let me speak of three which are closely connected, and of great importance—(i) The first is the literary and historical criticism of the Bible. It is impossible for most of us to decide with any confidence all the vexed questions upon which the debate of scholars is still proceeding, on the dates, structure, and authenticity of the various books. On certain points we may, without presumption, accept what seem to be the well-established conclusions of a reasonable and reverent criticism. On many others it is best to keep an open mind, remembering that the burden of proof rests with those who question tradition, and leaving critical hypotheses to the test of purely scholarly research and discussion. But we can and ought to determine for ourselves the mental attitude in which we stand towards the general question of Biblical inspiration and authority. The subject is obviously too wide and difficult to be even approached as part of a single lecture ; but at least, let me ask you not to assume an attitude which merely ignores, still less an attitude which repudiates, either the method or the main results of sane and responsible criticism. It is quite impossible for any thinking man to sweep them aside and refuse to consider them. If we do, we shall certainly fail to be interpreters of truth to the minds of our generation; we shall miss the opportunity which we are called upon to use. I shall return to this matter; at present I am only concerned to insist that we should clearly know for ourselves and be able, when the need arises, to express to others the point of view from which we study and accept the Bible.

(ii) The criticism of the Creed. Hitherto professedly Christian criticism has been mainly occupied with Biblical subjects; now there are many signs that, impelled by its Biblical studies, it is entering upon a criticism of the statements of the Creed. The discussions on the evidence for the Virgin Birth and the Resurrection are signs of a rapidly advancing tendency of professedly Christian thought. It is a tendency which looks for the basis of Christianity, not so much to the facts of New Testament history, the evidence of which is at least disputed if not uncertain, as to the experience of the Christian consciousness, the evidence of which is immediate, authentic and clear. The Christ of history retires into a more or less uncertain background, but the Christ of experience comes into the foreground with a convincing claim of His own. Now there is a certain degree of truth in this position. The consciousness of Christ in experience is itself a part of the fact-basis of the Christian faith. But it will be found that there can be no real severance between the Christ of history and the Christ of experience, that the former is necessary to account for and ultimately to preserve the living power of the latter. I am convinced that in our day we shall have to choose between regarding "the living Christ" as a mere spirit in the mind and heart of man (which received a singularly full expression in the life and teaching of Jesus), and Jesus Himself, son of God and Son of Man, still abiding in man in His own Divine Spirit ; in other words, between Christ as a human sentiment or aspiration, and Christ as a revelation of God, witnessed by the historical facts of the Incarnation, the Crucifixion and the Resurrection. In regard to this choice we must know where we stand. Let us indeed beware, as we watch this tendency growing, of the indignation of mere ignorance ; let us be slow to accuse earnest and faithful men of themselves denying the Incarnation, because they are doubtful as to the evidence of the Virgin Birth ; or of themselves denying the Resurrection because they are doubtful as to the accuracy of all the details in the Gospel narrative. Let us distinguish between what we may believe to be the ultimate issue of the tendency in question and its immediate meaning to the personal faith of men who are under its influence. But with regard to that ultimate issue we must determine our attitude and know the reason which compels us to adopt it.

(iii) The criticism of the Church, of its authority, its orders, its sacramental teaching. There was a time when the faith, and in a certain sense the claim, of the Church was taken for granted. That time is long since vanished. There was a time when ignorance as to the principles which distinguish the Church from other Christian bodies was common even among the rulers of the Church —an ignorance which met every summons to reform with sloth, panic, or obstinacy. May we not say that it was ignorance in high places as to the real principles of the Church, which caused the loss to the Church of England of the followers of John Wesley, and of the genius and saintliness of Newman? Let us remember these warnings of the past. In our own day the characteristic claims and doctrines of the Church are on all sides challenged. The fact of its mere "establishment" counts, and rightly counts, for little intellectually and spiritually; it is on grounds of intrinsic principle that the Church must be defended; and the challenge of principle is sustained and serious. The claims of the Church of Rome are being urged, and its attractiveness is commended, by every device which intense faith, controversial courage, artistic ingenuity, and social influence, can command. On the other hand, the Protestant communities can no longer be regarded as mere "non-conformists"; they represent, not a mere refusal to conform to the Established Church, but a positive and impressive ideal, both of Christian doctrine and of the true meaning of the Church. I would advise you, if you wish to realize the spirit and strength of what is called the "Free Church" position, to read the life of that great Christian and citizen, Robert Dale of Birmingham. It is into this atmosphere of challenge that we bring, not only the Gospel, but the Gospel as it is entrusted to us in the teaching and discipline of our Church.   We stand before men as the responsible and accredited teachers, not of Christianity in general, but of Christianity as it is conceived by the body to which we belong.   To sustain this part with any effectiveness, not to say with honesty, we must know for ourselves why we belong to that Church, and give our lives and our services in loyalty to it.   It is not enough that we may happen to have been born in the Church of England; that, desiring to serve God and our fellows, it was the natural course for us to be ordained in the Church of our baptism, or the established Church of our country.   The basis of our Churchmanship must be personal choice, based upon deliberate conviction.   We must have for ourselves before we can give to others, an answer, and a reason for our answer, to such questions as these: Why am I a Churchman?   What do I mean by my Priesthood and by the power which at my Ordination was

solemnly conferred upon me? What is the real
place of the Sacramental system in the Christian
life? Our answers may not be learned, we may
not as yet be always able to sustain them in close
argument, but at least they may and they ought
to stand, at the very outset, for some personal and
intelligent thought and choice.

You may think that these are very obvious and
elementary points, but speaking with some knowledge of the minds of men as they approach their
Ordination, and of too many clergy long since
ordained, forgive me if I say that if they are
obvious, they are also very commonly forgotten.
It is not our business here to discuss what answers
ought to be given to such questions as those which
have just been mentioned. I only plead that, whatever our answers may be, they should at least be
in a very real sense our own.

What we all want, then, is not so much detailed
learning, for that is a matter of talent and opportunity, as a clear and intelligent *attitude of mind*
towards the great questions of religion, but
specially towards those which occupy the minds of
men at the present day. How can we hope to
attain this attitude? To that question there are of
course many answers; the only one of which I
can now speak is this : we must bring our minds
into contact with minds greater and larger than
our own, with the minds of great teachers. For

F

most of us, and for the greater part of our life, this resolves itself into the duty and method of our own reading.

Let me add that when I speak of reading in this context, I mean reading the books of master-minds. If at the university you read merely your notes of lectures, or a few easy "cram books," in view of university or bishops' examinations; if at a theological college you read only fragmentary manuals of theology; if afterwards you read only in a hasty and haphazard way, in order to find some-thing to say upon a particular text or subject, then your mind is never aroused; the faculty of memory may be exercised, not the faculty of thought. But if you read some great book patiently and reflec-tively, then you will find that the great mind which is within it enters and stirs your own, and sets it to work. Time may efface the memory of particular facts or arguments, but it cannot efface that mental influence. You have gained an atti-tude of mind towards that subject which, even unconsciously, will survive. Let me take a few examples. It is impossible, doubtless, to remember all the arguments of Butler's great " Analogy of Religion," but if we have read it with any care, it is surely impossible to forget its characteristic point of view; its impressive insistence upon the limitations of human knowledge and the pre-sumptions of probability remains as a permanent endowment of the mind. Again, if we study the Gospel of St. John with Dr. Westcott, or the Epistles of St. Paul with Dr. Lightfoot, we shall probably forget their comments upon particular passages, but we shall never forget the lesson which they taught of the method of studying the New Testament, of the importance of each shade of meaning expressed by word, or even particle, of the discernment of the sequences of thought in the sacred writers. Similarly, to read such very different books as "The Atonement" or "Ministerial Priesthood" of Dr. Moberly, or the most pregnant and stimulating lectures of Dr. Hort upon "The Way, the Truth, and the Life," is to acquire for the rest of one's life a certain large and true attitude of mind towards the great questions with which they deal. There are few of us who can be in the strict sense of the word learned men, but we can all be educated men; and the mark of an educated man is the temperament, or, to use the word once again, the attitude of mind with which he approaches any subject.

Moreover, if the mind itself, by this fruitful contact with mind, has been exercised and strengthened, then, when it has for itself to consider and speak about these subjects, it will unconsciously work along the lines in which it has been trained. The actual thought or argument may be another's, but the force and vigour with which it is presented will be one's own. It will come forth with an impression of reality, and therefore will have some chance of going home with effect.

And once again, the habit of reading great books with care teaches two things of the utmost practical value. The one, what knowledge really means; and the other, as a consequence, what we do not really know. What injustice to the sacred cause of the Christian Faith would have been prevented, from what wounds at the hands of its own children would the Church have been preserved, if the clergy had only known the difference between knowing and not knowing. Let me quote the words of Dean Church.[1] "No man can know everything: but the men who influence the thoughts of their time are not those who try to know all things, but those who have learned one thing so well that they know and show to others also that they know *what knowing means*. 'Know as much as you can' should be our first rule. 'Never, as far as you can help, speak a word beyond what you do know' should go with it."

I plead with you, then, in your theological reading to form from the very first the habit of studying the best books, of always having a master-book in hand.

---

[1] "Sermon on the Twofold Debt of the Clergy: Human Life and its Conditions," p. 166. The whole sermon is one well worth reading and pondering.

The staple of our reading will be mainly and rightly Biblical and theological ; but do not let it be confined to that sphere. If we are to be the interpreters of God to men we must study the mind of man revealed in general literature, as well as the mind of God revealed in the Bible and the Creeds. You will find a fresh value in the old classical studies of school and college, if you remember, like the great school of Alexandria, that there you see the mind of man at its highest point apart from the revelation of God. You will note the differences, and still more the affinities, between the Christian and the pre-Christian outlook on the world, tracing in the latter the preparation of the Spirit of God in the spirit of man for the coming of Christ. In the literature of our own nation you will realize the heritage of thought and feeling which goes to make up the English character which we are charged to Christianize. In the literature of our own day, reflecting as it does the currents of thought, desire, perplexity, which surround us, you will keep in touch with the spirit of the time in which we are called to bear our witness. This literary sympathy will prevent us of the clergy from standing in a place apart, while the main stream of the thought and feeling of the time flows by unheeded by us, and therefore unheeding. It is, moreover, a real means of strengthening our own faith to watch the manifold ways in which minds moving on lines very different from our own are drawn somewhere and somehow within the spell of Christ. We are thus helped to realize that we hold on trust for the human race, not an illusion however beautiful, but a truth with which the mind and heart of man cannot dispense. All such general reading contributes to the freshness and confidence with which we hold the great truth of the Incarnation, that all the best movements of human life have their source and their consummation in the Christ. *Christus Vindex et Consummator Naturæ.*

II. Pass now to the intellectual equipment which we need in order to buy up the opportunity created by the second of our two special difficulties of the time, that is, the remoteness from religion of the masses in our great towns. Shall it be said that when we come to the place of hard practical work among ignorant and uneducated folk we need no longer trouble ourselves about our intellectual equipment?

On the contrary, there is a very special need of it, and this mainly in two ways : (1) The task of presenting the Faith to uneducated people demands two great qualities—simplicity and suppleness of mind. The teaching must be simple, but to be simple it must be plain ; to be plain it must be clear ; to be clear it must be vivid and real to one's own mind. And the teaching must be supple ;

able, that is, to adapt itself to all sorts of obstacles, often most perplexing and unexpected, of ignorance, perversion, misunderstanding, in the minds of the people. But it cannot be supple unless our own mind moves with the ease and sureness of a firm hold upon the truth which we are trying to teach. It is the best and most finely tempered steel which can be bent and twisted without breaking. A superficial or confused mind will fail to teach the Faith to the poor as signally as it will fail to commend the Faith to the educated classes. There is, indeed, no surer or harder test of intellectual grasp upon any subject than the ability to preach a simple sermon about it to plain folk. It is probably for this reason that so many clergy seem instinctively to shirk the test and fall back upon giving to the poor a "few earnest words" of exhortation. It would be scarcely an exaggeration to say, that of all the examinations which may await you for testing your theological knowledge, there will be none so exacting as your first confirmation class. "If you can make clear to *that* boy what his baptism means for him," said a good parish priest to his new deacon, "you need not be afraid of facing any Board of Examiners in the kingdom."

(2) There is one wish which lies very near to the heart of any man who works among the poor; it is, that he may be in the deepest sense their servant,

that by his service he may lift them to a higher and happier life. But to fulfil this great ambition of social service he cannot dispense with a real intellectual equipment. All day long and every day the parish priest and his fellow-workers are touching, and touching, so to say, at first hand, the most complicated problems of social economy. Each individual in the parish—that boy drifting into mere casual labour, that man thrown out of employment, that widow suddenly left to face life with her young children—each is the centre of a complicated web of moral and economic facts. To arouse within the poor the sense of self-respect and responsibility, to see how they can be so helped as to be enabled to help themselves, to restore and strengthen life entangled and crushed by hard conditions ; these are tasks which demand real knowledge and mental effort. The surgeon who undertakes to remove obstructions or restore life in any part of the body will make sad blunders unless he knows something of the relation of all its complicated organs. In our daily task of help-ing and serving the poor we shall make similar blunders, unless we know something of the con-stitution of the whole body politic. Every single case of relief involves an act of thought or judg-ment—right, if it helps to strengthen the resources of life in the poor we try to help ; wrong, sadly, often cruelly wrong, if it hinders them. We are

simply bad and faithless servants of the poor if
our acts of charity spring from mere sentiment or
good nature, and not from the careful exercise of
judgment based upon thought and knowledge.

But let me take a wider ground. A very special
opportunity of service, not only to the poor, but to
the whole community, stands open to the clergy
and their workers. It is this: There is no lack of
public interest and effort in the work of social
amelioration, but it labours under two great difficulties. (i) In the first place, public efforts, both
charitable and legislative, are often based upon
imperfect information as to the real lives and
habits of the people themselves. They are often
made by enthusiasts, who see only the facts which
they are anxious to find, or come in contact with
the people only in the aspect which specially
interests themselves. Over and over again we
find that laws are passed, or charitable enterprises
undertaken, which seem to be admirable until, often
in the most unexpected way, they are brought
up against some set of facts which were never
foreseen. Yet all the while there exists in England,
to an extent unknown in any other country, a body
of educated people, the parochial clergy and their
trained workers, knowing the people among whom
they live with thorough intimacy, watching their
habits day by day. Can it be said that this body
gives to the service of the whole community a

contribution of thought-out experience, of the results of investigation, at all proportionate to its opportunity? "They know so much," said an eminent public servant to me the other day, engaged in a special inquiry, "but it is so difficult to make use of their knowledge." He meant that the knowledge of the parish priest and district visitor, though intimate, was so little thought-out or held together by any method of study that it was of little use for others. It had not been set in order by careful, patient record and thought. Is it too much to say that there exists in the knowledge of the parochial clergy and their workers a body of experience of inestimable public value, if only it were made available for public use? They might be, as it were, a permanent commission of inquiry into the life of the people, settled in every parish in the kingdom.

(ii) In the second place, the best laws and the most useful institutions often break down in administration; and this is mainly because the people for whom they were intended do not know of the advantages they offer. To give only one instance out of many—how disappointing is the practical result of all the Public Health legislation of the last few years! Yet once again there exists in almost every parish this body of earnest and educated people, who have a welcome entry into the homes of all the poor, and have opportunities for giving advice and communicating knowledge —as to matters of health and domestic economy and opportunities of learning about them, as to the encouragement of thrift, and so forth—such as no other body possesses. Often, indeed, such advice is given, but by no means often enough. No one values more than I do (value is indeed a word so inadequate that it is almost impertinent) the devoted labours of the clergy and workers of the East End among the poor ; yet I cannot but confess that here is an opportunity which is only very imperfectly used ; and the reason is, want, not of zeal, or of capacity, but of training and knowledge.[1]

Forgive me if I seem to labour this point. I do so only because I am convinced that there *is* here a real and great opportunity of social service, which the clergy and their workers may use. Let me strongly urge at least these three points : (*a*) Every man who means to work, or is at work, among the poor, should qualify himself for his task by some knowledge of Economic History, of the Poor Law, of the Economics of Industry, of the Laws of Health and Housing, of the problem of the Unemployed. It is not, let me repeat, always possible to be learned in these difficult subjects, but it is always possible to acquire an attitude of mind about them, by which the lessons of daily experience can be made useful and fruitful. I wish

[1] See Appendix D.

that more might be done in this direction in theological colleges, and that every bishop would encourage his deacons and younger priests to attend lectures on social problems, or better still organize local centres for their common study. (b) Every parish priest ought from the first to make, and gradually to improve, some system of record, by which the results of his social experience can be gathered and tabulated. Of such records not the least important will be those in which the names and circumstances of all persons and families who have in any way received any form of help, or of relief, will be entered. Such records will be of infinite value to the parish itself, at every future stage of its history, and might often be of great advantage to the whole community. The mere keeping of them will be an admirable training in social knowledge. (c) Every effort should be made to train our bands of workers in this spirit of intelligent observation. By definite instructions and in frequent conferences we should try to make them our comrades in this enterprise, make them with ourselves a band of trained servants of the poor. I am certain that by taking more pains and practising more method about this branch of our work, the interest of visiting, so ready to flag, will be enormously quickened and sustained. Just as an even elementary knowledge of botany suffices to give ever fresh interest to the simplest country walk, so even an elementary knowledge of social economy would bring to the visiting of the dullest street something of the zest and stimulus of scientific inquiry. By such means the parish priest may become in a new sense the leader and the neighbour of his people, living in their midst, thinking out their problems for them, interpreting their real needs, pressing for reforms with a zeal tempered by knowledge, and above all, by his sympathy and his advice helping them to reform themselves.

I have spoken thus, I hope not at excessive length, of the intellectual equipment which we need in order to use our opportunity. Perhaps some have already made the inward reply, "All this is beyond me, it scarcely concerns me ; for I have no special intellectual capacity." To those who are still only looking forward to the Ministry I would make the rejoinder, Remember that a mind which may be dull and confused under the pressure of school and college tasks, sometimes uncongenial and out of touch with real life, often discovers new and surprising vigour when it is met by the problems of the life's work, when it comes into contact with living issues, and deals with living men and women. I can think of many a man who took a poor enough degree who is now working with a force, vigour, and intelligence, which mark him out as an able man. And to all

my brethren in the Ministry I would say, remember
that in the acquisition of this intellectual equipment, as in all branches of true life, it is the effort
that matters, not the achievement. The mere
stimulus of a high, true aim itself quickens the
mind into new activity. Our brains, like our
servants, degenerate when we treat them as mere
drudges, but improve when we associate them
with our best ideals.

Again, some one may say, and I know that
many of my brethren of the clergy would say it—
"This is all very fine and true, but for this intellectual business we have simply no time." No
one knows better than I do the measure of truth
in this plea, the ceaseless and dispiriting struggle
to break loose from the thousand entanglements
of parochial detail; but both my own conscience
and the example of equally busy men convince me
that "when there is a will there is a way." It
is this will to read that is so sadly wanting. Let
me implore you, to whom I more immediately
speak, to enter your parish with a fixed determination to make the time. You remember the well-
known criticism of a famous public man: "He
always lost half an hour at the beginning of the
day, and spent the rest of the day in running after
it." Of how many clergy is it not true that they
have lost the habit of reading in the first two
years of their ministry, and spend the rest of their

days in the futile effort to recover it? At the very
outset make, and ever after keep with all the force
of resolute conscience, a fixed rule of reading.
Nothing but the instinctive compulsion of settled
habit can resist the intrusion of all sorts of justi-
fiable occupations. Moreover, remember that
generally speaking the habits of a lifetime are
acquired before a man is thirty. After thirty
comes the period of futile resolves and impotent
regrets. Bring then to your ministry a just
estimate of the proportions of your work, and
never surrender it. Hold to the habit of spending
some part of each day in reading against all the
temptations of parochial zeal, and of the excessive
practical energy of your colleagues. You may
know that you are right if they are bustling about
while you are reading at home. The issue involved is simply this, whether your life is to whirl
around in a mere busy circle until it is exhausted,
or whether it is to move in a steady advance ;
whether, in fact, you are to be the master or the
slave of parochial routine.

But this matter of reading carries with it a
wider obligation. We owe it to our people ; we
cannot teach them unless we ourselves are busy
learners. What was the secret of Dr. Arnold's
teaching power? It was the vigour of his own
mental energy : "I will not give my boys to
drink out of stagnant water." Is it not, alas!

only stagnant water, a monotony of teaching out of which all freshness and vitality have gone, that many, even conscientious clergy, give their people to drink? Can we wonder that the people do not care for the taste of it? "Keep to your regular reading," Archbishop Temple used to say to his ordination candidates, "otherwise you will find that your preaching becomes stale, and your people will have found that out two years before you do." We owe this duty to our Church. We have lately been told that the characteristic of the English Church is its appeal to sound learning. These words stand for a great ideal in past history, but in our day of exaggerated practical energy are they not in danger of becoming an empty boast? There is here a real call upon us of *noblesse oblige*. The obligation is the greater and the higher because the fulfilment of it is left to our honour. Officially, the Church of England requires only the test of a University degree in any subject, or two years in a theological college, and the passing of two bishops' examinations; whereas the Church of Rome requires a course of theological study lasting four or five years, and the established Church of Scotland a course lasting three or four. The official requirement falls miserably short of the ideal of our Church. It ought to be a point of honour with us to make up the balance. Nay, we must go a step further still ; to neglect the habit of reading is not only to fall short of an ideal, it is to break a deliberate vow. Perhaps if we began to look upon our remissness as a sin, we should not be so glib as we are in making the often almost jaunty excuse of "I have no time for reading." At our ordination we were asked: "Will you be diligent in reading of the Holy Scriptures, and in such studies as help to the knowledge of the same?" And we answered: "I will endeavour myself so to do, the Lord being my helper."

G

CHAPTER VII

OUR Spiritual Equipment. The last chapter leads naturally to the thought of the spiritual, as well as the intellectual, equipment which is required of those who would "buy up the opportunity" of the Church of England. We cannot here treat this subject at any length, partly because its importance is so obvious that it ought to be unnecessary to emphasize it.[1] Within the limits of our plan I can only speak of it so far as it bears upon the effectiveness of our message to our fellow men to-day. I dare not speak of it in its bearing upon the saving of our own souls. Let me only ask you to remember that saying of our Lord's, one of the most terrible sentences in the New Testament: "Many will say to Me in that day, Lord, Lord, have we not prophesied in Thy Name? And in Thy Name have cast out devils? And in Thy Name done many wonderful works? And then

---

[1] Instead of enlarging on the theme, I would rather simply recommend the Rev. A. J. Robinson's little volume on "The Spiritual Life of the Clergy," published by Messrs. Longmans, in their excellent series of Handbooks for the clergy. It presents the matter with singular truth of spirit and aptness of language.

will I profess unto them, I never knew you : de-
depart from Me." It is the doom of eloquent
preachers and successful organizers and popular
clergy, who have neglected the maintenance of
their own spiritual life. Verily, what shall it
profit a man if he draw crowds, or acquire fame,
or "run" his parish with success, and lose his
own soul?

But it is of our work that we are speaking ; and
here it is, after all, mainly through our own
spiritual life that we are able to commend the
truth to our day and generation. Alike to the
educated and the poor, our message, if it is to go
home, to reach and touch and raise our people,
must come from that knowledge which is vision,
nay, which is deeper than vision, the knowledge
of Person by person. If our witness is to have
effect, it must be the witness of first-hand evidence:
"We speak that we do know," "That which we
have seen and heard." In our age, specially held
by the bondage of material things, we have to
convince men of the reality of things unseen ; and
the only testimony which can effect this conviction
is the testimony of life. Men will say of our word,
It is true, when they can say, pointing to our
life, It is lived. Of course, we all recognize that
the only tolerable basis for our ministry is the
reality of our spiritual life ; but alas ! how often
we forget that that reality can only be maintained

by deliberate effort, and reflection, and self-discipline. In our day, thank God, it is scarcely possible for any man of ordinary honesty to be ordained, who does not know something of real penitence, or prayer, or a sense of the divine call, or of the personal love and claim of Jesus. It is surely always with some such spiritual endowment that a man passes from the wonderful and happy day of his ordination into his first parish. But alas! how easily, how quickly, the freshness of it is worn away by the wear and tear of pressing routine: the youth

> by the vision splendid,
> Is on his way attended;
> At length the man perceives it die away
> And fade into the light of common day.

Ah, that fire of devotion and zeal by whose light the early vision stood clear before us, and by whose glow the early days of ministry were warmed! How many hard-working clergy know in their heart of hearts that its embers are dying out, that soon they will be fain to warm themselves at borrowed fires! How dreadful, alas! how possible, to come in from a day's parish toil to find the fire gone out in the hearth of a man's own soul! And as for the path of our progress, which ought at each stage to be "shining more and more unto the perfect day," rising higher in spiritual power and zeal—is there not a rebuke, the force of which the conscience of many of us must acknowledge in the Pope's dedication of a letter to Archbishop Baldwin of Canterbury : "Baldwino monacho ferventi, abbati calido, episcopo tepido, archiepiscopo frigido."

I cannot speak now of the moral slacknesses and self-indulgences, the roots of bitternesses springing up, which slowly but most surely destroy the spiritual life ; though I have before my mind, as every Bishop must have, the memory of many men, who, starting with the highest aims, have slowly drifted into sin, and seem to have lost even the elementary grace of conscience ; men who show that there is no bondage of sin more appalling in its pressure, and more remorseless in its tyranny, than that which holds those who are living in the midst of spiritual words and acts. Of these moral dangers I cannot speak, but let me ask you to think of three dangers to the spiritual life which inevitably beset all of us within the very sphere of a conscientious ministry.

(1) The first is the use of religious language ; to us it is a matter of official duty ; we cannot avoid it. It becomes habitual ; it rises instinctively to our lips ; it is always, alas ! it may become only, the language of our daily business. Its very ease and fluency is one of our greatest dangers; we must continually and severely test its reality in the crucible of self-scrutiny and prayer.

(2) Second, there is the influence of routine. Every day has its stated and official religious acts, its answering of letters, its interviews, visits, arrangements; they are all part of our work. Each one of them can justify itself to the conscience. But unless they are to become an entanglement, throttling our spiritual life, we must keep spaces of time clear through which the soul can escape from them and find its way out to God. "Mine eyes are ever looking unto the Lord : for He shall pluck my feet out of the net"; that is the only chance of life and liberty for the busy parish priest. Unless at times he resolutely drives the thronging details of parochial routine from the door of his spirit, so that it can fly away and be at rest in communion with God and things unseen, he will become weary, stale, dispirited, and deserve the epitaph : "Born a man, ordained a priest, he died a conscientious drudge."

(3) Thirdly, there is the ambition of activity. It is, perhaps, the special snare by which in these days the spiritual conscience of earnest-minded men is entrapped. Self, in the form of a passion for energy, is disguised, and therefore doubly dangerous. The spirit of the day is on its side ; the pace at which life is lived, the worship of outward effectiveness, the practical temperament of the Englishman, all favour it. But against this insidious temptation we must make our stand.

Let me quote the wise words of Professor Seeley : " In all professions, a man's first duty now is to renounce the ambition of becoming distinguished for activity ; a higher, calmer sort of activity must be arrived at—economy in energy, expenditure without waste, zeal without haste." There are enough and to spare in our English Church of men of energy ; I suppose there is no body of clergy in the world so energetic. What we need, and need sorely, is more men of God. In all this adulation of activity we are apt to think and act as if there was no such thing as the independent working of the Divine Spirit. We have all need of the rebuke : " Be still and know that I am God." It is only in this stillness of the soul that we bring ourselves into touch with the energy of the Spirit of God, and when *that* energy passes into ours, it becomes not mere activity, but power.

Finally, all this leads to a plain and practical point : if we are to work in the power of the Spirit, to keep our spiritual temptations at bay, and thus to impress men with the reality of things unseen, there are two supreme practical necessities laid upon us—we must make time to pray, and we must make time to think. Here, even more than in the matter of reading, we must look upon the plea " I have no time " as simply the voice of temptation ; for if we once persuade ourselves that we have no time to pray or think, but only to do, then very little of all that we do will be worth doing. Our work is ultimately spiritual; it is spiritual, not only in its motives, but in its aims and its resources. If we will not make time to pray and think, we part with the only power by which this spiritual work can be done. This matter is, therefore, in the strictest sense, vital and essential. There is a pregnant truth in the saying of Luther: "I have so much to do that I cannot get on without three hours a day of praying."

(i) First, then, we must make time to pray; and by prayer I do not mean our official and public acts of prayer, not even the hurried moments of private prayer, without which no man who is otherwise than a mere hypocrite can possibly begin or end the day. I mean the sort of prayer which was commended to us at our Ordination: "Wilt thou be *diligent* in prayers?"—the prayers which are part of the serious effort of life, for which we detach and reserve, not only real spaces of time, but real energies of the spirit. This is the prayer in which we hold communion with God and Heaven, and thus share the Divine life and mind and love. It is the prayer by which we lift all our concerns of work, our plans and wishes for our people, one by one, to God, and hand them over to Him, that they may be disciplined

by His will and filled by His power. Thus to
pray is indeed to labour, for this is the work on
which the success of all other work depends.
When I think of those in my own experience who
in their Christian ministry have wielded the
surest power and done the most abiding good,
I recognize that they were not the men of most
conspicuous ability or impressive energy, but the
men of whom I know that they were "diligent
in prayers."

(ii) We must take time to think; and by thinking I mean of course not merely working out our
sermons or instructions, but the thinking which is
deliberately set upon the realization of truth, when
the mind is absolutely and deliberately surrendered
to the Spirit of God in patient effort to *know*. Such
thinking is often called "meditation." I hesitate
to use the word, simply because there are many, I
know, who imagine that when one uses it, one
refers to a particular pious exercise which may or
may not be found edifying. I am not concerned
with the particular methods that may be adopted,
but I do insist with every earnestness which I can
command that the thing itself is of vital moment
to the clergy. It is a duty which cannot be dis-
charged without taking constant and earnest pains.
As Mr. Arthur Robinson truly says, "The hour
of meditation must be protected, as men were wont
to guard the well in the fortress." Here let me

repeat what was said before in another context: the only real protection is a formed and fixed habit; and if habits are to be fixed for life, they must be acquired before middle age. You will hear enough of this necessity of the pastoral life in after years, in every retreat you make, in every embertide address you hear, but alas! it is often in these after years too late. I beseech of you now to fix this obligation on your soul, and to hold to it with the utmost tenacity. It is through this habit of meditation that alone we can keep the inspiration of hope in the midst of disappointment, of tranquillity in the midst of difficulty, and of joy in the midst of toil. The man who goes forth to his work and witness from this "house of defence," brings to both, not only a quiet strength and a sustained ardour of spirit, but an unfailing impression of reality. The Truth, from Whose presence he comes, goes with his words and deeds into the hearts and lives of his people.

CHAPTER VIII

WE have now considered, however imperfectly, first, the general character of the two special difficulties of our time, which I have put before you as opportunities to be bought up by the Church of England, and the spirit with which we ought to approach them; and second, the personal equipment which we need for the task. I wish now to speak in greater detail of some of the definite means which we can use to fulfil our aim. In the present chapter I shall have the first of the two difficulties more specially in mind, that is, the current tendencies which act as dissolvents of religious faith and custom. In view of these tendencies, I desire to impress upon you the duty of being the *teachers* of your people.

Our main defence against these dissolving forces is the definite and intelligent teaching of the Christian faith. Their influence is chiefly due, as we have already seen, to widespread ignorance of what the Christian faith, as our Church believes it, really is. This ignorance among all classes is no doubt partly a result of the bias of the English

temperament, which is above all things practical.
It dislikes and distrusts doctrines which seem to
have no immediate bearing upon practical life ; it
is content with broad results in social and domestic
morality.   But though this is no doubt true, the
prevalence of this ignorance is a rebuke to the
English Church, and especially to its clergy.
When we consider the length of time during
which the Church of England has been entrusted
with the teaching of Christian truth to the English
people, the hold which it has had for centuries
upon the great public schools, and upon many of
the elementary schools, and upon the children
crowding its Sunday-schools, the fact which none
can deny, that very few Englishmen have an adequate conception of what the Christian faith as a
whole really is, can only mean one thing—that
the teaching office of the Church has been sadly
neglected.   It has been thrust aside by other
activities, sometimes practical, sometimes, let us
admit, ceremonial.   The very fact that we have to
deal with the anti-doctrinal temperament of our
race ought to have been, not an excuse for want
of teaching, but a very special spur to make
teaching clear, continuous, and definite.   Facts
will not allow us to resist the conclusion that
we clergy, as a class, have lamentably failed in
the discharge of our teaching office.   We have
either been remiss in any definite teaching at all,

or we have taught in a way which has not touched the life and mind of the people. There is no call more urgent in the present day than the revival and strengthening of this teaching office of the Church. The arrears of neglect are formidable ; the determination by God's help to overcome them must be in proportion patient and sustained.

This revival must keep two objects steadily in view, and never allow the one to be severed from the other. These are : definiteness and reality. The teaching must be definite. Christian senti- ment, undisciplined and uninstructed, has resulted in a widespread, vague, undenominational re- ligion. We have already deprecated the habit of undervaluing and even scoffing at what is called our common Christianity. It does represent a unity in the midst of so much depressing division ; it does witness to a common hold of certain great Christian facts and principles, for which we can- not be too thankful. But it becomes dangerous when it is set up as in itself the whole Christian truth, or even as a distinct and satisfactory form of religion. It is not only, as we Churchmen must believe, that it omits matters which are part of the Christian revelation, but also that it wants coherence; it is too flexible to be strong; it follows inevitably the lines of least resistance; it cannot be taught or embraced with any real enthusiasm of conviction. We shall only be perpetuating the vagueness of Christian belief, and therefore leaving it as a prey to the dissolving forces of the time, if while we eagerly make the most of any and every point of concord with all our fellow-Christians, we are afraid or ashamed to teach that definite Christianity which has been committed in trust for the future to the historical Church of Christ.

But, second, the teaching must not only be definite, it must be real—that is, in touch with the actual needs and thoughts and difficulties of men in each generation. That is a point on which we have repeatedly insisted in these lectures, and it must never be forgotten. One of the best definitions of true teaching is that given by one of the most inspiring of teachers, Edward Thring of Uppingham : "It is the passage of life, through life, into life." That is, the communication of a message, itself vivid with reality, through the living experience of the teacher, into the living experience of the taught.

1. Consider, then, our duty as teachers, first of all in relation to what we call the educated classes. Here there is surely abundant reason for searchings of heart. Education has advanced in almost every sphere except that of religion, with the result that as a whole educated people are still lamentably ignorant of the Christian faith and of the coherence of its different parts. Think of the

religious teaching given to the children of the
educated classes in contrast with the education
now given to them in any other branch of knowledge. Think of it even in contrast with the religious teaching given to the children of the poor.
I have often been struck with the difference here of
the standard of expectation. Does not the Church
seem to expect and take pains to secure a higher
standard of religious knowledge in the children of
the parish school than in the children of the rich,
and a higher standard of, say, attendance at church
or Holy Communion in working lads and girls
than in the girls of comfortable homes or the
young men at the Universities or in business? I
wish we could honestly reply that the reason of
this difference is the admirable home teaching
among the educated classes. It is true that in
almost every Christian household there are lessons
given of a sort — lessons chiefly in the form of
Bible stories and moral talks; but how vague
they are, how unmethodical, how seldom gradu-
ated so as to fit the growing intelligence of the
child! Is it an exaggeration to say that the impression of religion left by this sort of teaching
is that it is morality coloured by Christian sentiment? We know, thank God, that in many homes
that morality is both sound and gracious, and that
around that sentiment cling many of the tenderest
associations of life. I am not thinking or speak-

ing specially of these, the ordinary influences of a good home, but simply of the extent of clear and definite religious instruction; and that is extremely limited. Nor can we forget that even distinctively Christian influence is often absent from professedly Christian homes. It has been stated—and the fact seems most significant—by the head master of one of our great public schools that after careful inquiries he came to the conclusion that seventy per cent of his boys came from homes where there was neither the custom of family prayers nor any religious instruction of any kind.

But, we may say, the boys at least have their chance at school. Certainly there has been in the last twenty-five years an enormous improvement in the religious teaching of the public schools; but it has been an improvement, in the main, rather in the care and earnestness with which it is given than in the specific subjects of instruction. It moves still too much in the region of the kings of Israel and Judah, or the journeys of St. Paul, or the geography and history of Corinth and Philippi, too little in the region of the great doctrines of the Incarnation, the Resurrection, the Church, the Sacraments, and of their permanent bearing upon actual life. Is it not true that for the most part the force of the teacher is put into his moral teaching? We may thankfully acknowledge that that teaching is earnest, manly, and strong;

that working with the best influences of public school life, it sends thousands of Englishmen into every profession and every part of the world with a noble standard of honour and duty. But looking at our social and political life with candid eyes, can we say that it sends them out with a clear knowledge of the Christian faith as a coherent whole, or with a sense of loyalty to the Divine Society, the Church of Christ, at all comparable to their sense of loyalty to their school?

Can we wonder that when school days are over, and men come into contact with the dissolving forces of which we have been thinking, they should drift away from any definite adherence to religion, or to the life and worship of the Church? The spirit of inquiry, when it enters, finds the house swept and garnished, and takes to itself the other spirits of doubt or of indifference. Yet the pity of it is, that the average Englishman thinks that he has learned and does know his Christian faith, by what Dr. Liddon used to call "that innate knowledge of theology which is the inheritance of every British man and woman." He reads magazine articles, even, perhaps, the essays of Huxley; possibly some one puts the books of Samuel Laing before him. He is upset, or at least disquieted, by their arguments. It never occurs to him that it is not the Christian faith that they disturb so much as his own fragmentary and

H

uninstructed conception of it. Probably he never thinks of carefully reading any really first-class books on Christian doctrine ; he assumes that he knows it. It may give point and reality to these remarks if I venture to use my own experience as an illustration. I left Oxford, with I hope some knowledge of philosophy and history, and, though without any intention of being ordained, with probably a greater interest in religious questions than some of my contemporaries. I can remember as a layman in London taking part in interminable religious discussions, and criticising the doctrines and practices of the Church with the utmost confidence. Yet I know now that my ignorance of these very subjects was extreme ; I had never read any of the great classics of the English Church, yet I assumed that I knew all about it. And what was true of me was at least equally true of almost all the men who took part in these discussions.

If we turn for a moment to educated girls and women, I have often been struck by the fact that the naturally strong religious bent of their sex has only rarely been disciplined and strengthened by any definite and coherent knowledge of Christian doctrine. If they are clever, and interested in the literature and conversation of the day, is it a thing to be wondered at that their sympathy with the difficulties of the Christian faith is stronger than their knowledge of its real contents ? That while believing, often passionately, in the Christian spirit, they feel out of touch with the Christian Creed and Church? That the demands of their religious instinct should be attracted by new and fascinating forms of religion? Surely, then, it is clear that the religious instruction of our "educated classes," from the days of childhood onward, ought to be made more definite.

In this effort the Church, and especially the clergy, must take a more earnest and vigilant part. I cannot, of course, go into any details, but this at least may be said, the beginning must be made with the parents. The clergy, in their pastoral intercourse, and above all in their sermons, can give at least to them some real and systematic knowledge of the faith and the Sacraments. They can give them some basis for their own instruction of the children at home, and arouse in them a determination to demand a more careful and definite religious instruction for their boys and girls at school. The supply of such education will only come when there is a widespread and effective demand for it from the parents.[1]

Let me return then to the main point, that the Church of England, if it is to buy up its opportunity, must set itself to revive its teaching office in relation to the educated classes. The teaching must aim at definiteness; but it must also aim at

[1] See Appendix E.

reality; it must keep in touch with real life, and this mainly in three ways :—

(1) It must, of course, come from reality of grasp in the mind of the teacher; of that point I have spoken sufficiently in previous chapters.

(2) Secondly, it must appeal to the actual problems of life with which the men and women to whom it is addressed have to deal. There ought to be little of what I may call the dogmatic temperament even in our dogmatic teaching—the temperament which is content, and even ready to say of any doctrine, " take it or leave it, there it is." The school in which we are appointed teachers is the Church of England, and it is to the honour of the Church of England that it refuses to exercise an authority which is merely dogmatic and arbitrary. It offers its truth to the free allegiance of its children, encouraging them to think it out with their own minds. Thus our teaching, however definite, ought to be presented in a way which will commend its helpfulness to the truest instincts of life in our hearers. This amount of deference we can pay to the English practical spirit. We can recognize it by making the appeal of our teaching, not only to the understanding, but to the fundamental needs of human life. Let me give an illustration of what I mean. It is a striking letter in the Life of Tennyson,[1] from Professor Henry

[1] Vol. I, p. 301.

Sidgwick, a name of honour in the University of Cambridge: "What 'In Memoriam' did for us, for me at least, in this struggle, was to impress on us the ineffaceable and ineradicable conviction that *humanity* will not and cannot acquiesce in a godless world; the 'man in men' will not do this, whatever individual men may do, whatever they may temporarily feel themselves driven to do, by following methods which they cannot abandon to the conclusions to which these methods at present seem to lead." It is always to the "*man in men*," of which Mr. Sidgwick speaks, that we have to address our teaching. It is not elaborate apologetics or arguments, not formal disquisitions, any more than emotional exhortations, that educated men really want in our sermons; it is the clear, honest, intelligent presentment of our faith in its relation to the best desires and deepest needs of their actual lives.

(3) Thirdly, in our teaching of the educated classes, we must combine instruction in Christian doctrine with instruction in the habits and practices of the Christian life. Men must be led to see that if the truth is ultimately a personal thing, and the Creed a revelation of the way in which a Divine Person deals with human persons, it is only through personal intercourse with that Supreme Person that the truth can be realized or the Creed understood. They must be taught to

see that prayer and Sacrament are the means by which that intercourse can be secured; that these acts are acts of obligation, not dependent on our likes and dislikes, or the state of our emotions; and that on the faithful and dutiful observance of them depends the reality and the constancy of their religion.

The issue, then, is simply this: whether or not in the years to come the Church of England is to be able to justify the old and honourable boast that it retains the loyalty of an educated laity more fully than any other Church in Christendom. I know perfectly well that many of you will think "this is not a matter that directly concerns us; our work will be largely among the poor," or "we have not the gifts which are necessary to this special task." But let me insist that we are ordained to the Ministry of the Church of God before we are licensed to any particular parish; that therefore we can never escape our share of responsibility for the work and credit of the Church as a whole; that in our own, however casual, intercourse with individuals whom we know, with our equals and friends, or in work to which at any time we may be called, that responsibility as regards educated persons may become immediate and direct; that, therefore, none of us can treat this matter as indifferent. It will be a real disaster to English Christianity if the English

Church continues to devote the best energy of its best men exclusively to the thought and care of the working classes or of the poor.

II. Consider next our duty as teachers of the plain working folk of our parishes. Here the duty, though it is perhaps more generally recognized, is quite as urgent; much that has just been said applies equally to this branch of the subject. We must not suppose that our working folk are protected from the dissolving forces of which we have been speaking, and among them also these forces gain an easy victory over an uninstructed faith. A very short parochial experience will convince you of the quite extraordinary ignorance among even thoughtful working people of what the Christian faith and the doctrines of the Church really are. Akin to the Biblical difficulties of which I have spoken in a previous chapter, there is a widespread revolt against the crude theories of the Atonement which many believe to be the teaching of the Church. I venture to say that of the men who come to you in mental difficulty, for one who is perplexed by the facts of science there will be nine who are perplexed by elementary Bible stumbling-blocks, or by the doctrine of the Atonement; and you will almost be in despair that sensible men should have been able so long to think that their crude notions were what any intelligent Christian really believes. You will feel in your first talk with a working man about his difficulties, that in order to meet them you must begin to teach him the very elements of the Christian faith. There is still doubtless a place for the old lectures and debates on Christian evidences, if they are given or conducted by men who have special gifts, and, let me add, who themselves have some knowledge of what Christian doctrine is, as well as a knack of effective repartee in the exposure of free-thinkers. But the greater need and the greater good lie in the way of positive and clear teaching as to the Bible, the Creed, the Sacraments, and the Church. Men must know what Christianity really is before they can meet the difficulties which are alleged against it. Otherwise they will be at the mercy of clever writers, who set up their own notions of Christianity, and then with convincing ease knock them down. The best reply, for example, to the attacks of Mr. Blatchford would be a series of elementary instructions in the Faith which he professes to attack. This would enable men to see that he was often hitting vigorously in the air.

But teaching is needed, not only to repel assaults on the Faith, but to keep the Faith alive and growing. Unless we teach our ordinary parish people regularly and systematically, their own religion will become stale and barren. There are few things more fatal to a healthy Christianity than the torpor which is produced by continuous exhortations from the pulpit. As one whose duty gives him a wide experience of all sorts of varied churches, I can almost tell by the dullness or keenness of the congregation whether their pastor is mainly occupied in exhorting or teaching. The fact is, that our people are suffering from a surfeit of exhortations. Their religious life will wax strong only if it is fed regularly upon life-giving truth. I urge, then, that in whatever place our lot of work is cast, we must keep this ideal of our office steadily before us, that we shall be, please God, from the first to the last, the faithful teachers of our people.

CHAPTER IX

LET me now pass to the means and opportunities which we possess or may create for fulfilling the ideal of the Teacher. 1. First and foremost, there is *the sermon*. Here is our one great opportunity of teaching. No one can deprive us of it; none of our people, as they often complain, if they come to church at all, can escape it. For twenty minutes, at least once a week, we have our Church people at school. Let us scorn the silly habit which has become too common among our clergy, of belittling the importance of the sermon and the place of the pulpit. If in other days that importance was exaggerated at the expense of worship, there is no reason why we should now fall into the opposite extreme. Give a dog a bad name and he will deserve it; slight the pulpit and the pulpit will be slighted. Forgive me if I use some plain speaking on this point. It has been said, no less wittily than truly, that it is a miracle that the Church of England has survived its own sermons. Frankly, the condition of average preaching in our Church is most unsatisfactory. It is partly due to that excessive absorption in parochial routine of which we have already thought; partly to our neglect of reading; partly, no doubt, to a certain unworthy humility as to our own powers. But the main cause is, that we gradually acquiesce in a low standard, and as a consequence we do not take sufficient pains. We ought to feel when we begin the preparation of our sermons, that we are addressing ourselves to meet one of our highest and most responsible duties. When we enter the pulpit we ought always to say to ourselves, "Here I stand before these immortal souls with a message from the Most High God"; and to say to God, "Speak Thy message through my lips, O Lord!" It is often said, and said with truth, that it is the house-going parson who makes the church-going people; but this may become a dangerous half-truth. The other half is, that it is the preaching parson who makes the church-keeping people. I am sure that there never was a time in which people were more ready to respond to preaching. Any man who has anything to say from the pulpit, and who says it as an honest man speaking to his brother men, will always find willing and eager hearers. Magnify, therefore, your office as preachers, magnify it by earnest prayer and preparation and recollection of what it really means. And above all, for that is my immediate point, magnify it as your great opportunity for teaching the Faith.

Keeping within this necessary limit, let me say a few words both as to the matter, and as to the form, of our sermons. (1) First, the *matter;* let me plead for carefully thought-out systematic and *consecutive courses of instruction.* I know, of course, that, especially in the seasons of Lent and Advent, it is the habit of the clergy to give courses of sermons; but am I saying anything presumptuous or uncharitable if I suggest that the fare provided in these courses is often meagre and unsatisfying? If you were to study a collection of parish magazines, you would see the sort of courses which are sometimes proposed by clergy in need of a subject. I have seen such subjects as these solemnly put forth : "The G's of the Gospel" or the "Prepositions of St. Paul." You know the arbitrary and artificial collections of discourses, of which these are perhaps a not unfaithful caricature. I am thinking, not of such courses as these, but of the careful and methodical study, by parson and people together, of specific Christian doctrines or Books of the Bible. Let me give you my own experience as a parish priest. I do so simply in order to avoid talking mere generalities. God knows how miserably imperfect the attainment was; it is only the ideal which I ask you to share. At the parish church, then, there was always either on Sunday morning or Sunday evening, or both, and sometimes on a weekday as well, a definite course of instruction, for which the Vicar made himself responsible. I can remember on Sunday evenings a course of nine months, all too short, on the Sermon on the Mount; of three months on the Ten Commandments; of four months on the Creeds; and of several months on the Nature and Teaching of the Old Testament. I can remember on Sunday mornings a course of nearly a year on the Epistle to the Romans; of three months on the Epistle to the Ephesians; and other long courses, either in the morning or the evening, on the doctrine and ordering of the Sacraments; on the history and ideals of the Prayer-book; and on the History of the Church in the early centuries.

Does it seem to you that courses of such length, steadily maintained, must have been an intolerable burden, either to the preacher or to an ordinary mixed congregation, composed in the evenings almost entirely of working folk? I can certainly answer for the preacher. For him, it is not too much to say, it simply meant the difference between happiness and staleness in his preaching, between looking forward to the Sunday sermon with a sigh, and the old weary question, " What can I preach about now? " and looking forward to

it with the ardour of a man who braces himself
to a task which he knows is worth doing, and
which he is eager to do.   It gave an impetus to
reading, which otherwise would have been wholly
crowded out; it kept the mind fresh, in spite of
the pressure of parish work, and kept it centred
upon a definite subject, instead of being dissipated
and enfeebled by the mere necessity of much talking; it helped him to feel as he thought and
prayed over these great themes that the Spirit of
truth was with him in his efforts to lead his people
into all truth.   And I think I can answer for the
people.   The length of the courses never affected
the numbers of the congregation.   On the contrary, it helped to keep the people regular in their
attendance.   I cannot refrain from giving a lively
illustration.   A good petty-officer of the Navy was
ordered out to the Far East on some special service.   He told me he was very sorry to miss "the
course on the Romans," which had just begun.
Months after, he returned to the church; he heard
the text given out, " The Epistle to the Romans,
fifteenth chapter, such-and-such verse."   I saw
him turn and nudge his wife with a lively smile,
saying (as I learned afterwards), "Why, blest if
it isn't the same old course going still ! "

This consecutive teaching roused the interest of
the hearers and enlisted their own minds.   Many
would read beforehand the passage of Scripture

which was next in order, and try to make their own thoughts clear, before listening to the Vicar's thoughts. As one of them said to me, when a new course began: "We are saying to ourselves, Now we are off upon another journey." Nothing surely creates such a sense of community between preacher and hearer as this atmosphere of expectation. I speak from experience then, when I say, that if you will only pray, read, think, keep in touch with the lives and needs of your parish and bravely do your best, you will find that it is a real joy to be the teachers of your people.

(2) Secondly, a word as to *the form* of your sermons. There is one simple advice which holds good for your treatment of every class of hearers, educated or uneducated; it is, be simple, be direct, be natural. (i) *Be simple*. There is no subject which we cannot teach, if only we take pains to be simple in our terms. Avoid the use, as far as possible, of technical terms of theology; or only use them if you have first carefully explained them. To restore reality to the religion of the people, we have need continually to translate these technical terms into ordinary modes of speech. Avoid fine language, and all deliberately empurpled passages. A certain class of people admire such flowers and fancies, but it is a poor thing to make the Word of God pander to this taste; and such tall talking never gets beyond the

ears of the congregation, into mind, or conscience, or soul. I must quote the criticism which an old Yorkshire woman gave to me of a sermon just delivered in the parish church of Leeds by one of our most eloquent preachers—a whole volume on the subject of sermons could not go more directly to the root of the matter : "Nay, it were fine ; but it were all to be consumed i't' premises, there were nawt to be carried awaä." Remember again, what I have already mentioned, that in talking to the ordinary working-class congregation, you must get rid of two-thirds of your vocabulary. Straight, simple, Saxon words are the best. Let our deliberate aim be, not to be admired, but simply to be understood, not to gain a reputation for eloquence, but simply to say what we have to say as simply and forcibly as we can say it. After all, the only effective eloquence is the eloquence of felt sincerity of heart. No words, let it be said with deepest reverence, have had such an effect upon the world as those spoken once to peasants on the hillsides of Galilee by Jesus of Nazareth ; and they were of all words the most profoundly simple.

(ii) Be simple and *be direct;* fit the words of your teaching, not only to your own mind in the study, but to the minds of the men and women who will face you in the church. Watch and study these minds day by day, and speak straight to them. It is here that the teacher finds the value of his visiting. It is only daily intercourse with his own folk in their homes, in quiet talks in club, house, or vicarage, in shop or street, upon every sort of subject, that the parish teacher learns the ways in which the minds of his people work. Every visit in the weekday is thus a preparation for the sermon on the Sunday. The preacher who neglects visiting will always be preaching in the air. Always speak, not to men and women in general, but to *these* people, whom you know. Avoid, as you would in ordinary talk, everything stilted and conventional in thought and phrase; let them feel, not that you are preaching a sermon, but that you are talking direct to them.[1]

(iii) This leads at once to the third point. Be simple, be direct, and *be natural*. Avoid all affectations of voice and mannerisms of speech or gesture. We should aim at speaking with the natural urgency of earnest conversation. I cannot do better than use the words which the great actor Garrick wrote to one of his pupils who consulted

[1] I used to find it useful, as part of the training of some of my younger colleagues, to have discussions with them in which I assumed some character—say, of a Quaker arguing against the Sacraments, or of a reader of "The Clarion" in difficulties about the Bible, or of a dockyard labourer trying to understand the doctrine of Baptism—and compelled them to answer in a way which that particular character would be likely to understand. It was an exercise in direct teaching as useful to me as to them.

I

him about preaching: "My dear pupil,—You know how you would feel and speak in the parlour to a dear friend who was in imminent danger of his life, and with what energetic pathos of diction and countenance you would enforce the observance of that which you really thought would be for his preservation. You would be yourself. What you would be in the parlour, be in the pulpit, and you will not fail to please, to affect, to profit." That is the point; let us try to speak in the pulpit as we would if we were really dealing with a man on the things of his soul in our parlour or his. It is an easy thing to say, it appears to be a strangely difficult thing to do. Here is a young priest, a man naturally of admirable spirit, brightness and energy; at College he was felt to be a vigorous personality; in his district he is welcomed in every home, and has a wonderful influence over the men; in the club or on the football field he is the hero of the boys. He enters the pulpit and begins his sermon. But where is the man we know? He seems to have vanished. Some spiritless and conventional person has taken his place; a person speaking in a curiously pitched voice, saying words which the man we know would never utter, and apparently addressing some spectre in the wall opposite him. If only the man we know would return, and speak there in the pulpit with something of the straightness and the naturalness with which he speaks to his boys at the Confirmation class or club, and to his men at the fireside, then the sermon would not be a trial to him and to his hearers, but a living power.

Before we leave this matter of the sermon as the great opportunity for definite teaching, there is a possible misunderstanding to be removed. You will not suppose that I mean that all your preaching is to be of this character. It is true without doubt that no man can really teach the Faith or expound the Bible after honest prayer with any reality of conviction and earnestness of aim, without then and there appealing to and touching the heart and soul as well as the mind of his hearers; but there will always be a place, and a great place, in the pulpit for deliberate efforts to enkindle the spirit, to teach the conscience, to arouse the will, in short to convert men by the power of the Gospel. The missioner and the teacher within us must be the closest comrades. It was my own practice to break in upon the course of teaching with sermons having this expressly missionary aim. I know that the very specialness, so to say, of the occasion gave the words a special freshness and force; it was a real joy to lay aside the teaching and speak straight to the heart of the people with that conviction of the truth of his message which never comes to a preacher with such overwhelming power as when he pleads with them in the spirit of the very Love of God, and tells "the old, old story of Jesus and His love." I believe that such appeals will go home to the hearts of the congregation with all the greater force if they have not lost their freshness by constant repetition, and come only seldom, and then after very special and earnest prayer.

2.   The sermon, then, will be your chief opportunity of teaching; but it will not be the only one. On the contrary, *let the spirit of teaching pervade all the organizations of your parish.* Do not think it strained or fanciful if I suggest that the Church in the parish should be, as it were, a sociable School of Christian Learning, with its various departments and classes—a great continuation school, of both sexes, of all ages, and of all ranks. Besides the sermons in church, there will be the lectures in the parish hall, delivered either by the clergy themselves, or by invited lecturers, on the chief periods and episodes of Church History. To use words true in themselves, if somewhat cumbrous in the title of a society, the best method of Church Defence is Church Instruction. I remember with delight in my own parish, the crowds who, for four winters, attended lectures on the History of the Reformation from Henry VII. to the Church Revival in the nineteenth century. You will encourage lectures on Literature, as a means of helping your people to use aright the

faculty of reading which they possess, to know the difference between a good book and a poor one; and lectures on the wonders of Science, to show that the Church believes in all aspects of God's Revelation of His laws to man. You will have your system—shall I say?—of Training Colleges. There will be the training college for your Sunday-school teachers; that is, the weekly hour in which either you, or the most capable of your staff, undertake as a definite branch of work, to keep the teaching in the Sunday-school systematic, uniform in treatment and in tone. Wherever it is possible under the new arrangements, you will keep your influence over the young elementary school teachers in all classes of schools in your parish, helping them to make their preparation for their training at college as real in the matter of religion as in other subjects, helping them to make their own religious teaching earnest and thorough. There will be, as I suggested in a previous chapter, the training college of your visitors and Church workers, where you will study with them the economic problems of the poor. There will be the training college for your evangelists, the laymen who have some real vocation to witness for the Faith among their fellows; you will gather them round you in your study, and help them by simple teaching, advice, reading and prayer, to make their ministry an effective ally of your own.

Often in such simple gatherings, as you talk man with men, each under the influence of a true missionary spirit, you will have a wonderful sense of the presence and benediction of the Divine Teacher Himself. Not less important, there will be care for the training of those who are teachers by direct and Divine appointment, namely, the parents of your children. I am not entering any region of mere fancy, but only of a true and possible ideal, when I even venture to say that you can find a training college of God's teachers in the often despised Mothers' Meeting. What feeble and futile hours of listless sewing, and of insipid story-reading, might be spared to clergy and workers, if they only took pains to arrange their Mothers' Meetings in the spirit of this ideal.

I need not speak of all the different departments into which naturally the Church in the parish, viewed as a great Christian school, may be divided, such as the Bible-classes for men and women, arranged carefully with a view to really progressive education ; the classes in the upper standards of the Sunday-school arranged so as directly to lead up to Confirmation ; the gatherings of Communicants invaluable as opportunities, not only of maintaining devotion, but of imparting definite knowledge, without which devotion becomes sentimental and unstable ; the meetings organized by the Missionary Guilds, in which you try, not only to interest your people by stories of life and adventure in the mission field, but to make them understand the real problems of missionary work, and so at once to help the formation of an intelligent public opinion about the Missions of the Church, and to create an atmosphere of zeal and knowledge in which vocations for personal service can be realized.

But there is one opportunity of teaching, very real and often neglected, on which I must speak a special word. It is the visiting of the sick. I am not speaking of those who are dangerously ill or at the point of death, but of those who, either in sickness or during recovery, are in possession of their faculties. For them each visit ought to be a stage in an ordered scheme of Christian teaching ; it is a unique chance of laying the foundation of a stable faith. This is especially true of men, both of the wealthier and of the poorer classes. For the former there are now many books which can be left with them to supplement our own words ; but for the latter I earnestly wish that some one qualified, not only by devotion, but by what is in this context quite as important, a thoroughly human sense of what a working man can really take in, would write the books we need. We have tracts enough, and to spare ; we have devotional manuals for the sick, for the most part quite unsuited to this class of men. What we need is a short, pithy book of elementary Christian instruction. Further, there is a great opening for teaching in your prayers by the bedside; you can teach people how to pray. "Lord, teach us to pray," was the request of the disciples. I am sure it is the often unspoken request of many a sick person, touched at the time of his visitation by the Spirit of God. You can answer it best by your own example at his side; you can teach people by your prayers. I have often found that it was through prayer in the sick-room that one was best able to teach the truth about sin, the Atonement, and repentance. For this end, as for many others, I would strongly advise you to use in your sick visits simple and short extemporary prayers adapted to the circumstances and intelligence of the sick person. To produce a book, however good it may be, gives an impression of formality, makes the visit too much of a ceremony; fashion your prayers on the model of the Prayer-book, and of such excellent manuals as that of Bishop Walsham How, but let the form and language be your own.

Lastly, you may have perhaps thought that I have said very little about the teaching of the children. The omission is deliberate, and I have two reasons for it. The first is that I wished to restore the true balance of teaching energy. We should do more to secure the permanent effect of our instructions to the children in day-school and Sunday-school, if one tenth part of the energy and care devoted to them were given to the teaching of the parents. Sanguine persons, with a love of children, have a habit of saying, "Give us the children and we have the future in our hands." Alas! hard facts will not bear out this expectation. To a large extent we have had the children, and in the widespread ignorance and indifference of the mass of the people of all classes we see the measure of our success. The truth is we ought to say, "Give us the men and women, and we have some chance of keeping the children." Moreover, we have to learn in the sphere of religion as well as in the sphere of secular education, that half the labour we spend upon elementary teaching of children is lost, because we do so little in comparison to continue the teaching among growing lads and girls. If anything could compensate for the prospect of the Church losing its hold upon the elementary education of children, it would be the possibility that this might induce us to throw more energy and method into our efforts to keep our hold upon the lads and girls. But God forbid that I should seem to undervalue the enormous importance of teaching the children; and the second reason why I have said so little about it is, that the subject has been treated with the thoroughness which it deserves, and with a wealth of thought, illustration and suggestion, in the lectures delivered in Cambridge in 1903 by the present Bishop of Manchester, and now published under the title of "Pastors and Teachers." I would advise every one to get and read and practise the advice of that admirable book.

I have, then, been speaking of the organizations which will be simply part of the ordinary apparatus of your work. You must busy yourself with them just as inevitably as the barrister has to busy himself with his briefs or the clerk with his ledgers. They are, alas! only too apt to become a weariness to the flesh. They are quite capable of being so elaborated as to entangle and choke rather than help the religious life, both of clergy and people. It is quite possible for an admirably organized parish to be a sort of whited sepulchre covering dead men's bones. Everything depends upon the ideal with which you approach all this parochial business, and the spirit which you put into it. Keep the light of the imagination burning over it; have the courage resolutely to maintain an ideal far above what you can possibly reach. It is such an ideal of the parish priest as the teacher, and the Church in the parish as the school of the people, that I have ventured to put before you. The true idealist cares little either about the scale of his efforts or about the numbers to whom they appeal. You may fulfil the ideal of the teacher

and his school in the most obscure corner of a
grimy mining village. And as for numbers, even
if those who respond to your ideal be few, they will
be a nucleus of sympathy and co-operation around
you; they will carry some fragments of all your
labours into a far wider circle. But believe me,
let me repeat, your people will in time catch something of your zeal and answer it by their gratitude.

It is, therefore, with real envy that I think of
those who are still able, as parish priests, to make
the Church in their parishes a busy hive of teaching and learning. Is not this only carrying out
in a small sphere what the whole Church of Christ
was meant to be in the world, the school of divine
truth? May we not, therefore, here be assured of
the special aid of the Spirit of Truth himself,
who dwells within His body? Do not for a
moment suppose that the ideal is beyond you. It
is, indeed, beyond your attainment; it is not
beyond your reasonable effort. Remember that
what is now compressed within a single hour, you
will have, please God, many years of three
hundred working days, and ten hours a day, to
carry out. Remember it is only high and exacting aims which deserve and win the help of God.
Remembering this, look forward, not with appre-
hension and diffidence, but with real ardour and
expectancy, to the time when you will be placed
before your fellow-men as accredited and commis-

sioned teachers of the truth committed to the Church, and frame from the first the high ambition of being used in some measure, however small, and in some place, however humble, "to confirm the people's faith."

CHAPTER X

IN the last two chapters we saw that one great means of buying up the opportunity presented by the dissolving forces of the time was to revive and strengthen the teaching office of the Church.

In the following chapters we pass on to think of the second evil of the times which we are to regard as creating another opportunity for our Church, the existence, especially in the towns, of vast masses of people outside the influence of the Church altogether. You will remember that we have already tried to estimate the extent of that evil, to see the signs of hope which even there appear for our encouragement, and to consider the spirit in which we ought to face the task before us. I wish now to indicate in greater detail some of the ways in which we may hopefully try to discharge it.

There is a very real and most important connexion between this subject and that of which we thought in the last chapter. By careful teaching to build up and train the body of the faithful —that was to be our aim. You may think that this aspect of our work was over-pressed, that you were asked to devote so much thought and energy to "the perfecting of the saints" that you will have none to spare for "those who are without"; that in magnifying the office of the Church as a teacher we forgot its office as an evangelist and missionary. Undoubtedly we have great need to beware of this danger. It is quite possible so to wrap ourselves round with Church organizations that we gradually lose sight of the multitudes whom they cannot touch. The plea will always be plausible—" I have so much to do in caring for my own people, in teaching them, in visiting the sick and the members of the Church, in managing guilds and classes, that I have really no time for dealing with the rest of the people." The plausibility of the plea is strengthened by the pleasure of yielding to it; for the happiness of busying ourselves with our own Church people and children is so real, that often, however unconsciously, we come to shrink from the uncongenial, perhaps unrewarded, toil of attempting to overcome the huge surrounding mass of indifference. Nor are there wanting parish priests who come to justify the plea by saying in fact, if not in word, " The Church is here; I teach its doctrine; I perfect the ceremonial of its worship; I am ready to administer its Sacraments; I offer its services; I cannot be expected to do more." We must, indeed, beware of being satisfied with our own

people, still more of the profoundly false sacer-
dotalism of the last excuse. We must ever keep
the thought of the masses without upon our conscience. Night after night as I pass from some
bright and warm-hearted gathering of East End
Christians into the streets and see the crowds of
men and women, of lounging lads and laughing
girls, I feel intensely the burden of the question,
—After all, how few of these know or care anything for Christ and His Church? If the Good
Shepherd left the ninety and nine for the one that
had strayed, ought not we who are His representatives to leave sometimes the one for the ninety
and nine?

That is true, but we keep the proportion between
the two claims if we steadily remember that our
best chance of reaching the masses without is
really to train in the right spirit the faithful within.
That proportion is set before us in the words of
St. Paul, whose force is lost by the wrong punctua-
tion in our Authorized Version: "the perfecting
of the saints for the work of the Ministry." That
is the objective of all our training of "the saints"
—that they may become the ministering, the missionary body. We have for our continual guidance
the method of our Lord and Master. How intense
must have been His longing to find a response in
the mass of His own people, to say nothing of the
heathen world beyond! Yet with what care and

deliberation He concentrated His influence upon the twelve Apostles and the more immediate circle of His disciples. But when He had trained them to keep together, to realize their fellowship with Himself and one another in one community, He gave them the power of the Holy Spirit, and bade them go out into the world and make disciples of every nation. We have to follow His example. The very power and pathos of the plea of the multitudes is to constrain us with the greater earnestness to prepare the body of the faithful that it may go out and bear witness and make disciples. The call of those without is to be answered primarily by the motive with which we train those who are within. I shall return to this theme again, for it is really the pith of my message. I only mention it now, because it is the link between this chapter and the last. Suffice it for the moment to repeat that we are to make Christians better in quality in order that we may make them more in number, that we are to intensify the character of the Church in order that we may extend its influence; we are to strengthen the stakes in order that we may lengthen the cords. The two efforts are really only two aspects of the one task.

Place, then, before your imagination those crowds of people in our towns who live and laugh and work and weep and die as if the Christ and the

Church were no concern of theirs; and consider very shortly some of the ways in which we can try to reach them. Here let me say at once that there is the less reason for elaborate detail because the whole subject has been treated by the present Bishop of London with his incomparable freshness, terseness, and force in the lectures which he delivered in Cambridge when he was Head of the Oxford House: "Work in Great Cities." It would be mere folly to go over the same ground with heavier steps. I shall only attempt on certain points to supplement his experience with my own, and to treat the subject in the light of the general principles which we have taken as our guides.

Efforts directly religious. Let me say a few words on three of these: men's services, additional services in church, and special missionary efforts. (1) *Men's services* represent a very special movement of the last twenty-five years, and take a prominent part in the life of most town churches. They have passed through the stage of novelty and excitement, and we are now able to consider them in the light of long and varied experience. Let me offer you some hints gathered from a fairly wide field of observation. A clear and distinct objective must be kept steadily in view. Men's services are a means, not an end in themselves; like many others, this commonplace is

K

often forgotten. Let me put it in a blunt form : their main object is not to get the men into the services or the buildings, but to get them into the service and fellowship, of the Church. They are an evil if they are only regarded as a substitute, they are a good only if they are regarded as a preparatory stage, for the worship and membership of the Christian body. For the attainment of this aim there are at least five conditions which experience seems to show must be observed.

(i) The services ought to be under a *single influence and control*. I do not think that much good is done by bringing into the parish a succession of strange preachers to speak to the men. An occasional visit from some well-known preacher may undoubtedly be useful from time to time in giving new vitality to the service and in bringing the men into contact with representative churchmen. But the core, so to say, of the service must be the influence of a single man. I can scarcely think of any instance of a permanently successful men's service in which it has not been the special work of one man, of the vicar himself, or of some specially gifted curate. "What has been the secret of success in the Polytechnic movement?" Mr. Quintin Hogg was once asked ; and he answered, "Somebody's heart's blood." It was his own. The same reply must be given to the question, What is the secret of success for

men's services? There must be behind the concentrated prayer, effort, thought, teaching, influence of the will and mind of one man—watching
the men Sunday by Sunday, getting to know
them personally, establishing a connexion between
them and himself, dealing with them as their
known and trusted friend. It is this personal
interest which is the first and best link between
men and the Church. I feel this so strongly that
I would even say that unless there is in the staff
of the church one man who is specially able to
take this part, it is better not to attempt a permanent men's service at all. No man can do
everything, and those who are not qualified for
this method of reaching the men may be well
qualified for others. Beware of the temptation, so
common in these days of conventional parochial
organizations, of having a men's service simply
because it is the thing to do. Whether or not
it is the thing to do depends entirely on whether
or not there is the man who is capable of doing
it. Is anything so tedious and unedifying as a
men's service which has no spirit of its own,
where a special preacher addresses "a few straight
words" to a company of somnolent men on a
Sunday afternoon scattered about an empty
church? It is a good custom, year by year, to
review the parish organizations, and in the case
of those which have lost reality and vigour to

order a massacre of the innocents. I am certain that if a men's service becomes lifeless and spiritless it ought to be killed before it wastes away. No amount of advertising, or of brass bands, or of solos, will keep it alive when the vital power, by which alone in my experience it can retain its influence, has once gone—"somebody's heart's blood," the influence of a single man.

(ii) The men's services ought to be *continuous*. This is essential if the object is not to get the men to hear special sermons, but to bring them into real touch with religion. There must be continuity of time and place. My experience is that it is best to hold the service every Sunday throughout the year, with a considerable interval in the summer months. But there ought to be also continuity in the subject of the addresses; the men ought to be in some way led on from point to point, however slowly and with whatever politic digressions, on some definite road, not kept moving aimlessly round and round in a circle of popular subjects. Of course, if the object is at all costs to gather or keep large numbers, the best means of attaining it is doubtless to provide a weekly or monthly sensation. But what is the use of that? We must always be beaten in the competition of sensations by other bodies less hampered by traditions such as ours. In any case, once the appetite for sensations becomes jaded, it soon betakes itself elsewhere for change. If the object be a permanent impression, some continuity of subject is essential. My own practice for five years in Portsmouth was to have conferences for men every Sunday afternoon from October till May, addressed with scarcely an exception by myself alone. And for these months the subject was continued, practically without break from Sunday to Sunday. We had long courses of such subjects as "The Difficulties of Religion," "The Duties of Christian Citizenship," "The Lessons of the Great Leaders of Religion of the Nineteenth Century," "Outlines of the Life of Jesus," "Common Errors about the Bible and the Doctrines of the Christian Church," and the like. What was the result? This : that beginning with an audience of, say, seven hundred, we kept a steady and continuous nucleus of from three hundred to two hundred men. Now, it is in that nucleus of men that there lies the real hope and permanent value of the services. It is they who respond ; it is they who come nearer to truth and to Christ ; it is they who are deepened in spirit and strengthened in character ; it is they who become candidates for Confirmation and members of the Church ; and it is they who in turn become witnesses among their fellows.

(iii) The men's services ought to be *sociable*. The men are standing at the porch of the church ; let their first impression be that there is there a

hospitable welcome and a real brotherly spirit with
in. My own plan in dealing with the better sort of
artisan was to have the men's meeting or conference
in a hall as the regular gathering, and then, at
stated intervals, a special service in church. You
can be much more free and flexible in subject and
manner in a hall than you can fitly be in church.
You can be as unecclesiastical as possible, for you
are there mainly as a man speaking to your brother
men. Moreover, in a hall you can give the men
liberty to ask questions or offer criticisms. The
questions may often be foolish and wide of the
mark, and the criticisms be most perverse and
irritating ; but the great thing is—you show that
you are not afraid of either, and that gives men
confidence, not only in you, but in the Church
and cause which you represent.

Our object is to gain the trust and confidence of
working men by taking our place frankly at their
side, and if the price we must pay is the chance of
being sometimes in an awkward corner it is not
too dear.

(iv) The men's service ought to be promoted
and managed by *a committee of the men themselves;* this is indispensable to its success. Begin
with a company of men of whose keenness you
are assured : show them that you look to them for
their help, that you trust them to bring others,
constantly meet them and prove by your super-

vision of their efforts that you value them. Ask their advice about times, subjects, and the general conduct of the services.

(v) Lastly, the men's service must be *followed up* by intercourse between the leader and the audience. Once men get interested in the service they will readily give their names and addresses as members. Do not press this point too much, but let it come naturally, chiefly through the influence of your committee. You will find the list invaluable; it will be the means of bringing you into touch with many men whom you might not otherwise know. It will give you a natural introduction to them. I can think of many men thus known who proved to be full of interest and of stimulus to oneself, men through whom one gained valuable knowledge of their class, of its desires and its difficulties, some of whom became most useful henchmen of the Church.

I have been led into greater detail in speaking of these men's services than I intended;[1] the excuse must be that in this branch of our work, as in so many others, its success depends upon capacity for taking pains. To hold a men's service is a thing well worth doing, but this only if real thought and care are given to doing it well.

(2) I pass now to the question of *extra Prayer-*

[1] See Appendix F.

Book services in church. I have no hesitation in giving them a prominent place among the means by which we may hope to reach the people in our great towns. We are bound to provide the services of religion contained in our Prayer Book, and to provide them with loyal fidelity and zeal. We are bound to see that Matins and Evensong are said daily in church. On this point let me urge that no plea except the compulsion of absolute necessity ought ever to be allowed to justify exceptions to the rule. After all that has been said and written on the subject, I have never met with any argument in favour of its suspension which rises above the level of an excuse. "All priests and deacons are to say daily the Morning and Evening Prayer either privately or openly, not being let by sickness, or some other urgent cause." This is to each of us a solemn personal obligation. It is one of the few acts of spiritual discipline which are required of the English clergy. The faithful observance of it gives a tone of strength, of discipline, and consistency to our whole life and ministry. It is a daily reminder that we are men under authority; it fosters a sense of comradeship binding the clergy together. It enables us to realize, that even when we are alone we are still the ordained representatives of men before God, on their behalf offering the daily sacrifice of prayer. This being so, what can be more reason-

able than that we should discharge this personal
obligation within that common House of Prayer,
that meeting - place of the Divine Society—the
Parish Church? Daily service in church gives
an opportunity to any of our fellow-members to
join us; even if they do not or cannot come, the
fact that the parson is seen to be faithful in his
prayers impresses his people much more than he
knows; and the regular tolling of the bell is a
quiet reminder to all the neighbourhood of the
things unseen and eternal.

This digression may be permitted as indicating
one sphere at least of loyalty to the Prayer Book;
but beyond this, when we use the services
appointed in the Prayer Book, let us keep to
the order and the language in which they are set
forth. There is not space to deal with the per-
missible exceptions to this rule; it is sufficient
to emphasize the principle. In the public and
stated acts of the Church not only our parishioners,
but any other persons who may be present, have
a right to expect that the language of the Prayer
Book, and of the Prayer Book only, shall be used.
We have no right to set ourselves up as arbiters
of its fitness or unfitness. Indeed, so careful and
purposeful are the principles and the structure
of the Prayer Book services that to maim them
is really to change them. The custom of clipping
even Matins and Evensong, though it may have

an Act of Parliament to warrant it, is most unsatisfactory. When Matins and Evensong are
offered, let them be given : in my judgment, if
they cannot be given as they are, it is better
frankly to substitute some other form of service,
which at least would not be a maimed rite.

Once again, it is the experience of every parish
priest that even the most simple and ignorant of
his faithful people learn to love and prize their
Prayer Book. Even though they cannot put
their thoughts into words they find in its ordered
sequence, its familiar rhythm, its gathered associations, a quietness and tranquillity which at once
soothe and strengthen them in their toil. They
come to feel at home in it, to regard it as their
own, with something of that love with which they
cherish all those familiar possessions which make
up what they pathetically call their "little home";
things that abide, that preserve old memories,
amidst the changes and chances of their life.
They often show a touching family pride in
realizing for themselves and showing to others
that they know their way about their Prayer Book.
Surely this is a feeling which we ought in every
way to encourage by our own loyal use of the
Book. By taking every pains to explain its meaning and unfold its beauties we should help our
people to prize their Prayer Book, to regard its
teaching as their common heritage, and its Psalms

and Prayers as their common speech, as members of the Family and Household of God.

I have spoken thus about the Prayer Book in order that what is now to be said may not be misunderstood; every word which follows is based upon a profound gratitude and veneration for the Prayer Book, upon a belief that it is unique in its power of training and deepening both mind and heart. This is only to say that the Prayer Book justifies its claim to be a manual for the faithful; its ideal is not, and never was, to be a means of attracting or interpreting the worship of those who are without. It is obviously, indeed professedly, unfitted to be a missionary agency. Its whole structure, the arrangements of its Psalms and lessons, the style of its language, presuppose habitual use and what may be termed a certain trained Church temperament and intelligence. We have already more than once noticed that so far as the mass of our modern city population is concerned the beautiful sixteenth- and seventeenth-century English is practically a language not "understanded of the people." The non-church-going working man, induced by persuasion or curiosity to attend Evensong, finds much as men found three centuries ago in "the number and hardness of the rules called The Pie" "that to turn the book only is so hard and intricate a matter, that many times there is more business

to find out what should be read than to read it
when it is found out." Women appear to be less
sensitive in this matter than men; men are intensely shy if in a public place they do not know
what to do next. As a good man said to me of
his first Church service: "I never knew where
they were or what they were doing; it was down
one minute and up the next, and such a turning
of books as never was. I felt hot all over to be
such a like fool in a public place." Unless either
regularly, or from time to time, we offer services
of a more simple and elastic type, I do not think
we shall succeed in winning those people to church
whom it is at once most difficult and most necessary
to win.[1]

Further, the religious life with all its varied
needs cannot be, so to say, shut up within the
limits of the Prayer Book. Those who have
opportunities of private reading and devotion use
them naturally to fill up the gaps which the Prayer
Book leaves; but for the vast majority of our
working folk such opportunities scarcely exist. It
is in their church that they ought to be able to feel
that their wider needs and more personal desires
are understood and expressed. Meetings in church
for simple Intercessory Prayer, in which all the
simple human wants and pleas of His children can
be laid before their Father in heaven; special ser-

[1] See Appendix G.

vices for guilds, for mothers, for boys, for Friendly Societies, and other similar groups of parishioners; services of common preparation for the Holy Communion; simple mission services with much use of the softening, cheering, teaching influence of hymns—these are some of the means by which the church can be made, not merely a place in which set services are held, but a home full of a warm and kindly family life. I cannot but believe, that thus to accustom people to come to our churches for other purposes than the appointed Prayer Book services would lead to their finding it natural to enter them privately at any time of the day, for quiet and prayer. Surely nothing is so sad, nothing seems to show so clearly that our people have not yet found in their church a home, as that in districts so overcrowded and noisy the people should so seldom seek in their own churches the space and stillness and rest which they so sorely need.

This, then, is our ideal—to make the church God's Room in the parish, where all His children can feel themselves at home, and extra Prayer Book services are necessary for any attainment of it. We do not want a supplementary Prayer Book compiled by authority to provide such additional services, for it is their very essence to be flexible and adapted to the condition of each church and parish. But our use of them ought to be controlled by three principles, which are indeed involved in our loyalty to the Church which we serve. (i) They ought to be always in accordance with the mind of the Church as it is expressed in the Prayer Book. They are to supplement that book, not to override or innovate upon its teaching. (ii) However simple and spontaneous, they ought to be always true to that reverence which befits the House of God, and to that spirit of order, quietness, and restraint of extravagant emotion or sentiment which befits the Church of England. (iii) They ought always to have the consent and approval of the Bishop of the diocese. We may confidently hope that our rulers will cordially approve of such services as conform to the principles thus laid down. Under authority all the services of the Catholic Church must be, but it is of real importance to the Church of England at the present time that that authority should be exercised not only to restrain, but also to encourage. Doubtless there is a risk that through the door of these extra services, teaching and practices alien to the spirit and standards of the English Church may here and there be introduced, but it is a risk which must be run : it is, after all, a risk involved in the movement of a living body. The Bishops of the Church can never allow themselves to become a mere ecclesiastical police. Their work is not only to "keep the Church in order," but to keep it in life; and order when it degenerates into mere uniformity is inconsistent with life. You cannot cramp the energies of a living body within the letter of an ancient Act of Uniformity. The Bishops' authority, which in this matter cannot be questioned, ought to suffice to forbid services which are inconsistent with the principles of the English Church; but the encouragement of such services as those of which we have been speaking, loyal to Church teaching, tone and authority, is of vital moment to the Church of England in its effort to reach the masses and win them for Christ and His Church.

(3) *Special missionary efforts.* Our great towns seem to be in possession of the forces of sin and indifference, and our churches in their midst are like little fortresses tenaciously held for the cause of Christ against overwhelming difficulties. It is hard enough work for them to hold their ground, to keep the garrison loyal, and here and there to win individuals back. Doubtless this quiet and determined pertinacity will in the end have its victory, but from time to time in the long spiritual warfare there must be special assaults in force against the enemy. The work of the Church must be aggressive as well as defensive. It is of these more aggressive efforts that I wish now to say a few words. (*a*) First, into the important question of *parochial missions,*

usually so called, we have not time to enter fully. It is indeed useless to lay down rules, for experience shows that no fixed rules are possible. Each parish priest must decide for himself whether the time is ripe for a mission; each missioner must decide for himself in each case how to conduct the mission. The less hampered he is by any doctrinaire methods the better. He ought to be ready at a moment's notice, owing to some shift in the campaign, to change his methods altogether. But there are some results of experience which may be recorded. Of late years, as we all acknowledge, parochial missions have been mainly successful in deepening and strengthening the religious life of those who are already attached in some degree to the Church. Doubtless in many cases this has been due to a want of true evangelical fire and fervour, to the confusion between a revival and a teaching mission. But it will be a mistake in every case to look upon this result as a disappointment. It may be one of the ways in which God is making it plain that before any great ingathering of the indifferent can take place the Church itself, acting with the zeal of all its members, must become a great missionary agency. A mission may be in the truest sense successful if it kindles in the faithful the fire of missionary zeal, if it compels them to give open witness for Christ, if it brings some of those who are standing on the outer fringe of nominal Christianity within the circle of real religion and devotion. In so doing it has not only brought many souls nearer to Christ, but it has made the Christian body in the parish a more compact spiritual force, which the Holy Spirit may use to accomplish His work in time to come.[1] It is war which tests the quality of a nation's patriotism, draws forth its latent capacities of self-sacrifice; and in the life of a parish there is nothing like a mission for arousing, testing, and enkindling the patriotism of the Kingdom of God. If therefore a parish priest feels that he has around him a company of the faithful on whose prayers and services he can rely; if he feels that many of His own people have reached what may be called the clinching point, the stage where the next step is open decision and witness for Christ; if he sees in a wider circle others brought by various influences to the threshold of the Christian profession; if he thinks that he can follow up a mission when it is

---

[1] I can think of one parish in East London where the effort to induce even the men who belonged to its clubs to take any part in the life of the Church had been long and difficult. A mission was held, after careful preparation and prayer. The clubmen were asked to join it. To the surprise of the clergy, they responded, not only by resolving to close the club at the time of the mission service, but by joining the processions in the streets. The sight of a procession of some three hundred people, largely men, not only gave a visible sign and stamp to their adhesion to the Church, but profoundly impressed the whole parish.

L

over ; then he has come to the situation in which he can rightly ask—Ought I not to have a parish mission ?

(*b*) Secondly, with regard to another aggressive effort, namely, *open-air services* and street preaching, a word of caution may be spoken. We say, "If the street will not come into the Church, let us take the Church into the street," and there is truth in so saying ; but in many places, certainly in East London, there has been too much, rather than too little, mere street preaching. Not long ago one Sunday evening in a single street I counted no less than eight street-corner services, each of them conducted with obvious zeal, and attracting nothing but the most languid interest. What with the Salvation Army, the Evangelistic Bands, and the efforts of enthusiastic individuals, there is a danger of the people becoming Gospel hardened.[1] By all means let the Church go into the street, but let it do so with every attainable circumstance of reverence and solemnity, always after special preparation and prayer ; and let those only speak who have some special gift. Let it be an event which touches the imagination and compels the attention of the people.

[1] As an illustration I may mention an incident in my own experience. I was speaking in the street in the course of a mission in the East End. I noticed two typical "costers" lounging up. They listened for a few minutes as I spoke of the appeal of God's Love on the Cross. Then one said to the other, "Come along, Bill, it's only the same old gag" ; and they lounged away.

(*c*) Thirdly, I pass on to another aggressive method, which has not been sufficiently tried, and which might be of great effect—I mean a *united evangelistic effort* undertaken by the Church over a wider area than the parish. No one can deny that the best and most telling work of the Church of England has been done by the parochial system ; but that system, like all others, may become a fetish, and there are not wanting signs in many spheres of the evils of this idolatry. It tends to make the Church itself, as well as its clergy, parochially minded. In this matter of arousing the indifference of the masses, of breaking in upon it by a solemn and sustained challenge in the name of Christ, there is need for the common effort of the whole Church over a wide range. I am not speaking of the combination of parochial missions in some town or centre, a method of very doubtful value, but of the combination of several parishes in one single missionary effort.[1] The Church in some town or rural deanery might engage the largest central hall within its area, secure one or two mission preachers of exceptional power, and set all its parochial agencies to work to bring the people together. We are all apt to look askance at the great central undenominational missions ; but their defect lies not in their main idea, but in the teach-

[1] See Appendix H.

ing which is given, in the sentimentalism of their methods, in the exaggeration of feeling, and in the absence of any means of drawing those who may be impressed within the strengthening bonds of Church fellowship and discipline. These defects we can surely be trusted to avoid ; the main idea may well be followed.   There is always, and rightly, an inspiration and encouragement in a great crowd ; it impresses the imagination ; it has a responsiveness of its own to waves of influence. Let the Gospel be preached in all its simplicity, but let it be the whole Gospel, the Gospel which tells of the love of God uniting man to Himself by the Sacraments and the fellowship of the Church ; let stress be laid upon the need of every soul attaching itself, for the sake of its newly-aroused life, to the body in which alone that life can be nurtured and trained ; let each parish keep in touch with those in its own area, whom its workers have brought to the mission, or known to have been influenced by it.   If these conditions were fulfilled, such combined mission efforts might have a power far greater than that of separate parochial missions in winning the ear and, it may be, the souls of the indifferent crowd.   Surely we cannot bring ourselves to confess that our Church is so crippled by parochial jealousy, so rent by party divisions, that it cannot *as a body* fulfil the very primary purpose for which it exists—to proclaim the Gospel of the Kingdom of God and to draw men within it; that it cannot *as a body* obey the very first command addressed to it by its Lord —Go ye, teach, make disciples.

A combined mission—is it not, after all, another phrase for the Church itself? Remember that it is to the body going forth and making disciples that the great promise is given: "Lo, I am with you alway." It may be that when our Church girds up its loins to such common efforts it will discover with joyful surprise the reality and the power of that Presence in its midst. Divided we are only men, united are we not Christ Himself?

This thought leads us to the root of the matter: Apart from Me, our Lord warned us, ye can do nothing. It is Christ Himself who must still come into our cities preaching the Gospel of the Kingdom of God. If His Spirit be not in our words and methods they will fail. We have in recent years gone through an epoch of wonderful increase and development of the methods and machinery of the Church. In the matter of mere organization there is perhaps little that we have to learn; we have come to the point where further movement will be not advance but only restless activity, unless we are filled with the Spirit. "Be spiritual, be spiritual, be spiritual," was the thrice-repeated plea of the late Lord Selborne in an address to the clergy of Wales; and our own experience of the very energy and eagerness of the Church proves that it is the most literally practical advice which can be given. The year 1905 ought to mark a memorable stage in the history of our English Church. The Archbishops and Bishops with united voice and with special solemnity bade the Church wait upon the Spirit of God, and entreat Him to come and revive its spiritual life. Whether that appeal is to prove the mere pronouncement of a platitude, or the herald of a new Power, depends upon the continuity and importunity of our prayers. God's Will to grant we know, but we know also that it is conditioned by our will to pray. He has taught us that it is the persistent and importunate prayer that alone secures its answer. The Bishops' appeal at Whitsuntide, 1905, will fail if it be regarded as limited to the offering of prayers at that particular time : it will succeed only, but then surely, if it be regarded as the beginning of a new epoch of earnest, united, continuous prayer to, and dependence upon, the Holy Spirit of God. Let us look for the answer not only, not chiefly perhaps, to any special "revivals" as they are called, but rather to the endowment of the normal activities of the Church with a new power to reach and win the souls of men. It is out of the very dry bones of our Church life that the breath of the Spirit of God can create an exceeding great army.

CHAPTER XI

So far we have been speaking of directly religious efforts to touch the indifferent masses; let us now go on to think of some *methods indirectly religious,* but intended to bring men within the influence of religion.

1. First and foremost among these let us at once place the *regular visiting of the people in their homes.* The phrase "house-to-house visiting" has ever expressed an old and honourable ideal of the English parish priest. It has become the fashion in these days to question both its possibility and its usefulness. I have even heard of clergy who openly speak of it as something beneath the dignity of their priestly office. Let us admit, as we have already done, that sometimes the proportion which it ought to have in the scheme of work has been somewhat exaggerated; let us admit, as we must, that the constant shifting of the population in towns makes it often most disappointing; let us admit that in many large parishes where there is but a small staff it can represent only an ideal. But from its place

as an ideal, which we are trying honestly to
realize within the limits of our powers, let no
difficulties and disappointments dislodge it. In
this, as in other cases, we can only do our best,
but that at least let us do loyally and faithfully.

For (a) such visiting is a real test of pastoral
courage and fidelity. Nothing makes such hard
demands upon the natural man : nothing brings
so sure a reward to the conscience. I know well
how hard it is to set out, day after day, at the
appointed time, to face in some new street the old
trials of the door shut in one's face, or of the
rejection of our overtures of friendship. There
is perhaps nothing in any sphere of life which
hurts the spirit of a man so much as to knock at
the door of a house with a genuine desire to give
his friendship and sympathy, and then to be
treated as if he were a tradesman's tout. It hurts
not only his pride, but the best thing he has—his
disinterested desire to be a neighbour and a friend.
No wonder that the natural man shirks the task
and readily accepts the plausible excuses ever
ready to hand. On the other hand, I know also
that we never conquer that daily reluctance, never
return from a courageous afternoon's or evening's
visiting, without knowing in our conscience that
we were right, that somehow we are better men
and truer priests because we went. The motive
which sends you out, even the rejections you may

suffer, will give you a very real sense of fellow-ship with your Master's Cross, with its love and with its reproach. And, alas! it is not too often that this sense of reality is vouchsafed to us, the professed servants of the Cross.

But (b) apart from this reward of conscience, faithful visiting brings real, though less direct, rewards to our work. We have already dwelt upon its priceless value in giving us first-hand knowledge of our people as they are. But, further, we are learning more and more clearly every day that the raising of the people depends ultimately upon the raising of the people's homes. After all, home influence is of all others the most telling and the most permanent. Even the remnants of home-life left to many of our poorer folk have a power in them all their own. Whatever hold you may get upon individuals, upon the child in your school, or the girl or boy in your clubs, will be weak and uncertain, unless it is linked on in some way to their homes. You must get the oldest and deepest influence in life on your side. There is a very real danger lest our clubs, our classes and guilds, and the like should lose touch with the homes of the people; they ought to be a fabric of influence built upon the foundation of the home. That is why it is essential that the parish priest should know and be known in the homes of all his people.

(*c*) Lastly, abundant experience shows, that it is through the disinterested care of a brother man that there comes to the indifferent most simply and directly the thought that they have souls worth caring for, and a Father in Heaven who cares for them. No such thoughts are stirred in them by the parson who is content to offer his services in the church and to look after his own faithful people only. He is doing his own business, and the man in the street is not concerned with it. But when he finds that the parson, in spite, perhaps, of his own first rejection of his visits, repeats them with patient and good-humoured pertinacity, he begins to think out what it means. As a man said to me once : " At first I thought you wanted something out of me, but when I found it was only myself you wanted I thought there must be something in me worth wanting." Every thoughtful parish priest can think of many wonderful opportunities which would have been missed and lost for ever unless he had persevered in unpromising visits. Let me give two : they will press my point more effectually than any words of mine. The keeper of a low public-house had repeatedly scorned the parson and all his ways and refused to see him. The parson was told he was ill ; it seemed to him hopeless to offer a visit, yet he did ; and after a time the man consented to see him. The parson only told him the story of the prodigal

son : the final result was that the man himself
before his death made a full confession of his sins
and received the Holy Communion with every
sign of true faith. His wife was confirmed, his
children sent to church and school, and the nurse
who had attended him was confirmed and became a faithful communicant. Again, a dockyard
labourer had long refused to let the parson into
his house. " He had no truck with parsons," he
said. But the visits were repeated, and at last the
man fell ill and consented to open his door. And
the result ?—that he, too, before his death made his
confession, received the Sacrament of his Lord's
love and forgiveness, and when he was asked
" How about the end ? " was able to say : " Well, I
feel just like the kids do the night before they go
for their excursion." Believe me, you can never
tell what opportunities lie waiting behind closed
doors, nor what issues depend upon your venture
visits.

All this may seem to many of you advice so
obvious and commonplace that it is scarcely worth
giving ; but, alas ! I know from my own experience,
I can see in the work of many good men, how
easy it is to forget it. Once again let me plead,
Set the old-fashioned house-to-house visiting
before you as an ideal to which you will be faithful ; if it can never be completely realized, yet it
ought never to be withdrawn. When you see long

streets of monotonous houses before you where you can count on your fingers those which contain people who care for you and your Church, never let your thought become: "I have long since given up the attempt to visit these people"; but rather let it always be: "There is my task still calling to me; O God, give me courage and faithfulness to stick to it."[1]

2. *Clubs* for men, lads, and girls have now become so inevitable a part of parish life that they cannot be passed over in considering methods by which the Church seeks to reach the masses. It is plain that visiting the homes, all important as it is, cannot be the only link between the Church and the daily life of the people. Under the conditions of modern towns the men, lads, and girls who are at work all day cannot be expected to spend all their evenings at home. We may lament, but we must recognize, the fact. Let us do all we can, as I have said, to encourage the home-life of the people, but it must be done by other means than attempting to persuade the men, lads, and girls to remain in the evening shut up within the narrow and noisy limits of the family living-room: this would be to attempt

---

[1] On the whole matter of parochial visiting I would refer the reader to the admirable volume on "Pastoral Visitation," by Canon Savage, in the series of "Handbooks for the Clergy," published by Longmans, Green, and Co.

what is neither possible nor desirable. Left to themselves, the men will betake themselves to the public-house, the lads and girls to the streets or to the music-hall, when the working day is over. It is here that the club steps in. Little need be said on this subject of clubs, because I can refer you on this as on other kindred matters to the ectures delivered in Cambridge on "Work in Great Cities" by the present Bishop of London, who, when he was head of the Oxford House, might have been called the "King of Clubs." I can only supplement on one or two points what he has said.

(*a*) Clubs have now, so to say, passed the period of sanguine youth and entered the period of middle-aged reflection. Inevitable disappointments have led in many quarters to something like a reaction. The chief difficulty has been the vexed question of religious tests. On the one hand, if there is no compulsion in the way of attendance at religious services or Bible-classes, it seems very difficult to permeate the club with any religious tone at all; on the other hand, if some such compulsion is exercised, it is difficult to prevent the clubs from being restricted to the faithful few, or to prevent the attendance at the religious service or Bible-class from becoming unreal or unworthy in its motives. There is scarcely a town parish in which at some time or

other, in some form or other, this problem has
not been acute. The main conclusions after some
degree of careful observation seem to be two:
(i) that, after all, the success of a club depends
mainly on some personality at work within it; (ii)
that the vital point in regard to religious influence
is not the religious requirements, but the size, of
the club. If the number of its members makes it
possible for those who manage it to be in intimate
personal touch with each individual member, then
regulations about religion are a secondary matter.
The only really effective religious force is personal
influence at the head and heart of the club. On
the other hand, if the numbers are allowed to
become so large that such personal influence becomes impossible, then no amount of religious
regulation will be effective. The point of supreme
importance is that no success should tempt you to
enlarge your club beyond the limits of real and
continuous personal influence. If you keep it
within these limits the question of religious rules
is simply a question of tact, of your knowledge,
so to say, of the moral pulse of the members.
Only, even in cases where no religious obligations
are laid upon the members, let the direct link
between the Church and the club be plainly set
forth; let the rules against bad language, betting,
and gambling be strictly kept; let there always
be some special Bible-class or service which the

members know to be in some sense their own ; let there be no false shyness in inviting them to come to it and use it as their own. Make great use of the men, lads, or girls on whom you can rely as trying in their own lives to stand for the cause of religion. Encourage your communicants to share and leaven the life of your clubs, and discourage them from standing apart in respectable or "churchy" superiority.

A club kept true in tone will always be a real link between the Church and the life of the people, and a leaven of healthy moral and religious influence in the parish.

(b) I have already spoken of the great chance which the clergy have of taking a lead in continuing the education of the people.[1] The clubs are an opportunity ready to hand which I do not think we have used with sufficient courage and patience. Without doubt it is a great thing to raise and refine the social instincts of the people, a great thing even to teach them how to play. I know well by experience how games can be made to develop strength, manliness, and self-control in a lads' club as they do in a public school. Anything which brings healthy joy into the life of the people is a gift of God. But, after all, there are pleasures of the mind as well as of the body, and the lives of lads and girls, especially of the better

[1] See p. 19.

sort of working folk, can be wonderfully enriched and gladdened by some knowledge of books, or some skill of art or handicraft. Persevere in every effort to reach the minds of the members of the clubs; even if only a few respond to your efforts, these few will be well worth teaching. I cannot but think that the Nonconformist bodies do more in this matter among the young men of the tradesman and skilled artisan class than the Church, and I have come across many instances of thoughtful young men who have, for this reason, been attracted away from their Church. It is of vital importance that the Church in every way should show itself eager for the intellectual as well as for the spiritual and moral progress of the people.

3. There is one special means by which the Church can keep in touch with the best life of working folk to which I would call special attention. It is by identifying itself closely, in every parish, with the great work of *the Friendly Societies* and other agencies for promoting thrift. The men engaged in this work are the very salt of the working classes; whatever their attitude towards the Church for the moment may be, they are the men who are most akin to religion; they are the champions of the cause of self-help, self-control, self-respect among the people. Every year is making it more clear that the great alternative on

which the future of the mass of working people depends, is the alternative between thrift and drift. Let us back the friends of thrift with all our interest and influence. The means are many —such as opening our Parish Rooms for meetings of the Societies, instead of leaving them to meet in the public-house, the stronghold of the greatest enemy of thrift ; organizing branches of them in our parishes ; encouraging our children from the earliest years to invest their pennies in them ; placing their representatives upon our Relief Committees, and so forth. By so doing we shall do more towards permanently helping the poor than by any amount of charitable doles. In any and every way let us make the men who stand for thrift realize that the Church regards them as its allies and comrades in the great cause of raising the people and helping them to raise themselves.

CHAPTER XII

WE now reach our last and, indeed, main point, the point which I most desire to impress upon your minds—that the special opportunity which the Church has at the present time of attracting the people is to exhibit itself as a society, a brotherhood, of common life and service. I have already spoken of this opportunity in general terms.[1] Let my last words be to commend it to you as a great and inspiring trust.

1. First of all try to permeate the whole life of the parish with *a sociable and brotherly spirit.* Let it be felt that the Church is a happy and hospitable household of God. Even the most ordinary incidents of your Church life may be made symbols—sacraments if you will—of this spirit. Thus, the parson's hand-shake at the close of the Sunday service becomes a symbol of family union in the common home. The "Social" becomes the means of reminding all classes of parishioners that they meet on a common ground, as members of the highest Society on earth. The entertainment

[1] See pp. 53, 54.

restores the cheerfulness of the family gatherings of olden times. The very Parish Tea is a reproduction, under the conditions of modern life, of the Agape of the primitive Church.[1] Even the "Sale of Work" is a call for the common efforts, gifts, and talents of the members of the one family. These are incidents of parish work from which you cannot escape; you may find them merely wearying, even resent them as distractions from your proper task; or you may find them fresh and stimulating opportunities of realizing what Church life was meant to be. All depends on whether you bring into them the light and inspiration of a great ideal.

Moreover, let us do our utmost to make people feel that the society that thus welcomes and cheers them is not merely their own parish community but the Church itself—the Divine Society of which they are, or may be, members. The shifting of the population, the vanishing of families just when he has got to know them, is the great worry and disappointment of the parish priest in the town; but we have done something worth doing if we have trained our people while we had

---

[1] I know of one parish where this true idea is literally carried out. A special feature of the Dedication Festival is the Communicants' Tea on the eve of their great corporate communion. It begins with the reading of the gospel: hymns are sung, the people sitting, during its course. Yet the whole atmosphere is thoroughly bright and sociable.

them in this conception of the Church : they will carry it with them and look upon their Church wherever they go as at once their mother and their home.

2. Secondly, let us try to fill the Church in our parish with the spirit not only of a common life, but of *a common service*. Try to make every one who in any way enters within it recognize that he must take his share in its activity, in the work of the Kingdom of God. There is a very striking suggestion in Mr. Booth's summary of conclusions about the religious life of London which is well worth our pondering : There might be, he says, a great change in the attitude of working men towards the Church, if instead of approaching them with the question—What can we do for you? we rather approached them with the question—What can you do for us? It is indeed one of the great encouragements of work in towns to find how ready and willing people are to render this service, if only they are made to feel that it is wanted. If it is not given, the reason is almost always that it is not asked for, or that the asking has not been followed up by signs of real interest and sympathy. I know the reply often made—"It is so difficult to find work for people to do." It is; but it is one of those difficulties which are made to be overcome ; and it is wonderful how the inventiveness of a real enthusiasm for the ideal of

common service can overcome it. We must first of all get rid of the idea so natural to us amid all the traditions of our office in England that we ourselves are indispensable to all the work of the Church. From the very beginning of your ministry keep the ideal, not of "running," still less of driving, but of leading, your parish; seeking not so much to manage it as to train it to manage itself; not so much to do work by your own activity, as to get work done through the inspiration of your own example and influence. Then try for each of your people—especially, let us say, at the time of their confirmation—even for each man who shows his wish in some way to help you, to think out the question: In the light of their circumstances and abilities, what can this man, woman, lad, or girl do? The resources of ministry in the body of Christ ought surely to be as many and varied as the needs of man. There are always the ministries of teaching, of assisting in the services of the Church, as singers in the choir, servers in the sanctuary, sidesmen in the body of the church. There is opportunity for abundance of service for young men and women in the routine work of Sunday-school or Catechism. One of the reasons why these institutions often fail is that sufficient pains are not taken about them, and the clergy have no time to take pains. But beyond these obvious lines of work, ask some of your business men and tradesmen to keep the parish accounts; ask your leading working men to sit on your relief committee ; ask your artisans to be the painters, the plumbers, the carpenters of your buildings ; ask your communicants to become the sponsors for the children of careless parents ; ask your best and keenest men to be, as it were, the travellers for the great business of the Church amongst their fellows; ask and train the most spiritual and gifted men to be your parish evangelists ; ask the aged and those who are laid aside by long sickness to be the parish intercessors, one of the highest and holiest of ministries. Ask with keenness and tact, and believe me you shall have, often "in good measure, pressed down, and running over."

To keep what is given we must show that we value it and trust it, a thing easier to say than to do. We must refrain from petty criticism and interference; we must remember that these workers are not working for the clergy, but for Christ and His Church. Alas ! we know only too well the shipwreck of service often achieved by the parson who ties his conscience to his personal whims, and considers that nothing ought to be done except in the particular way in which he himself would like to do it. The best leader is the man who makes his followers feel that he is their comrade.

Is it not true that the real work of the Church, the extension of God's Kingdom, is not done because it has been too long left to the clergy and other official workers to do it—perhaps because the clergy have been too eager and masterful in attempting to do it themselves? The conception of the Church as a Brotherhood of Service has become lamentably unreal. It has been truly said that the Church of the majority is indeed the Church at rest; we have to make it the Church at work. Certainly we have come to the point at which, if real advance is to be made, the reserves of the laity must be called out. I am persuaded that there are great resources of ministry waiting in these reserves. It is, I believe most firmly, the special call and opportunity of the Church in the present generation to find and use them. In this context may I call attention to the aims and methods of "the Church of England Men's Society,"[1] a body created by the late, and commended to the Church by the present, Archbishop of Canterbury; a body which, in humble but earnest faith, seeks to promote and sustain this conception that the "true Churchman" is, and ought to prove himself to be, one who prays and works for the extension of the Kingdom of God? Surely such a federation of Churchmen throughout England and the Empire, pledged to be true

[1] See Appendix I.

to this ideal, would be a great power in transferring that ideal from the region of theory to the region of fact. Whether it is to be met by these, or by other means, let us be convinced that here lies a great opportunity for the Church of England to present itself, as, in words already quoted, "the living and many functioned brotherhood working in the power of the Spirit."

3. It would seem to follow that if the Church in each parish is to possess a common spirit and fulfil a common service, it ought to find some place for *common government*. There is force in the retort of the laity to the clergy, felt even when it is not expressed: "If you ask us to take a greater share in the work of the Church, ought you not to give us a greater share in its government?" The Church of England ought indeed to adapt itself as far as it legitimately can to the democratic conditions of English life; but let me rather put it, that the Church of England ought to adapt itself to the conditions required by the recovery of a true Church ideal. Therefore I would urge, so far as the point still needs urging, that there ought to be a real Church Council in every parish; a *real* Church Council, by which I mean one that is frankly representative of the laity. A council nominated by the vicar, or coopted by its own members, is better than nothing, but it is still in the nature of an extension of the

parson himself, or of a superior "set"; it is not fairly and expressly representative of Church people. This character can only be given by election. The vexed question as to the proper qualifications for this lay franchise is still under discussion, and it is not yet possible to foretell what the decision may be. It is at least earnestly to be hoped that we shall not be asked to accept any franchise which is not in some sense spiritual in its basis. It would be disastrous to make any attempt to revive a franchise based upon merely secular qualifications; this would mean attempting to revive and to perpetuate for the future a mere relic of an abandoned past; it would be not to revive but to contradict the ideal of the Church as the community of Faith, Life, and Service. There was a time when the Church of England could be described as the whole body of citizens "in its religious aspect," but that time has gone beyond recall; we may deplore, but we must face the fact. You cannot found a future for the Church of England on a conception of Churchmanship which is a mere anachronism, any more than you can raise a new tree out of a dead stump. The Churchman now must be in any regulations for self-government, what indeed as a mere matter of fact he is, not a ratepayer, but a baptized and professed member of that religious body which is known as the Church of England. So long as

the matter is still in the stage of experiment I
cannot but feel that we would do well in our own
parishes, as I did in mine,[1] to make the membership which carries the franchise with it, the membership which is given at baptism, professed at
confirmation, and maintained by communion. If
the authority of Convocation should decide on a
wider basis consistent with the spiritual character
of the Church, then we can loyally submit to it,
and the councils elected under a wider franchise
will follow the traditions and spirit already existing in councils elected by communicants.

But without further pressing the matter of
the franchise, what I am at present concerned to
plead is, that we should honestly endeavour to
give our laity some share in the management
of Church affairs. The limits imposed upon a
Church Council by the fundamental principles of
the Church must be carefully marked out and observed. The parson cannot consistently with these
principles be responsible to such a body for the
way in which he exercises his own ministry of the
Word and Sacraments ; even in matters of ritual
he cannot do more, though if he is wise he will
not do less, than consult them. But in regard to
all matters concerning the wider ministry of the
body of which we have been speaking, there will
be ample room for their counsel and decision.

[1] See Appendix K.

Doubtless it will be often difficult to persuade some ardent members that after all there *are* fundamental principles which distinguish the government of the Church from the government of other religious bodies ; but the ignorance of men on such subjects is largely due to their long isolation from any responsible share in Church management, and will be best removed by bringing them within it. Doubtless, too, you will often find the remarks of some of the members very trying to your pride, your temper, and your patience. But after all, you must expect perversity, obstinacy, and self-confidence among good laymen as well as among good clergy ; and it is better far that criticism should be spoken out publicly before the clergy where it can be met and answered, than whispered privately behind their backs, where it breeds secret misunderstanding and discontent. In this, as in other matters, let us "be all for the open air." He who believes that he has a true ideal to work out will be very patient with the hitches and delays in his experiments. And for ourselves, any discipline is wholesome which prevents us from yielding to one of the besetting temptations of our order in England— the love of having our own way, and the belief that somehow Church principles are involved in our having it. Always put before yourself as a solemn warning of what good men may become—

the spectacle of the little parish despot enthroned on the sense of his own importance, and treating all criticism as treason against his sacred office. We are to be the leaders not the lords of God's heritage.

We have thus set before ourselves as the ideal of the Church in our parishes the vision of a fellowship, a comradeship, of spirit and of service. You may think that in so doing we have wandered from our immediate subject—how to reach the masses of the people. Not so; my whole plea is that this is the sort of Church which alone can achieve that end. The day has long passed when the Church of England could rely on its historic prestige, position, and privileges. We live in the better, at least the more bracing, day in which it must stand on its own merits. It must commend itself among other religious bodies by the warmth of its corporate spirit and the worth of its corporate service. It must be a Church which in the presence of these other bodies is only the humbler because of its wider responsibility to the nation; only the more tranquil and charitable because of the security which it prizes as a branch of the historic Catholic Church; only the more patient because of its ancient title. The privileges which it most values must be the spiritual privileges which it accepts as a trust from its Master, and these it will rather keep for the deepening of its own life than proclaim in disparagement of the life of other bodies. It must seek to gain its influence not so much by the assertion of its claims, as by the width and faithfulness of its service. It must quietly and steadily keep before its mind the words of our Lord, "He that is greatest among you let him be as the younger; and he that is chief, as he that doth serve . . . I am among you as he that serveth." Let our English Church, then, be a body, a brotherhood, standing forward in the midst of the hopes, the energies, the problems, the sorrows of English life in the attitude—quiet, ready, resourceful—of one that serves. Thus by its own attractiveness reflecting the Divine attractiveness of Christ, it will surely draw many out of the desert of indifference into the household of faith.

We have now reached the end, not indeed of our subject, but of the time available for its treatment. Let us by way of summary review the journey we have taken together. I asked you to consider two special evils or difficulties of the days in which our ministry is to be fulfilled, namely, the dissolution of definite faith, and the alienation of the masses from the life and worship of the Church. I asked you to look upon these, not faint-heartedly, but hopefully, as in themselves creating opportunities for reviving the ideals and calling forth the resources of the Church of England. We reviewed in the case of each of these evils its general character and influence, and the spirit in which we ought to meet it. We considered the mental and spiritual equipment which we must possess if we are to acquit ourselves honourably in this enterprise—a mind kept vivid and real by continuous study of the Bible, of great books, and of pressing problems; a spirit kept true to the refreshing and empowering Spirit of God by earnest meditation and prayer. We then considered in greater detail the lines along which we may hope to realize our opportunity in the face of the tendencies which are dissolving definite faith. For this end we are to revive the teaching office of the Church, and to teach with clearness, simplicity, and sympathy with the special needs and problems of our own generation. In the face of the remoteness of our city populations from religion, we are to make our methods of religious influence free and flexible, adapted to the real wants and capacities of the people; we are to make the Church itself a ministering and missionary body; and, above all, we are to seek to present it to men everywhere as a brotherhood possessing a rich common spirit and fulfilling a corporate service of Man. By working faithfully along these lines we shall be understanding what the Will of the Lord is in asking us to serve Him in this generation; we shall be "redeeming the time, because the days are evil."

There are, of course, many other characteristic evils of the day of which we cannot speak ; but I venture to hope that the point of view with which we have regarded those which have been before us may help and encourage us in meeting others of which we have made no mention. Let us have the faith to regard each as creating not a mere difficulty to depress, but an opportunity to use. The evil, for example, of our distressing divisions calls for the special quest of charity and the more earnest hold upon the truths which still unite. The evil of the social condition of the poor calls for common thought and effort and the strengthening of all the influences which make for self-respect and self-control. The evil of that materialism which is becoming the disease of our Empire calls for a deeper sense in the conscience of the English Church of its imperial responsibility. Every evil of the day is a call to the Church of Christ not to bewail the time, but to rise and redeem it : "Wherefore lift up the hands that hang down, and the feeble knees."

I close with the prayer—for you to whom ordination to the greatest service in the world is still a prospect of the future, and for us to whom it brings a memory at once stimulating and solemnizing of the past, and on whom it lays an honourable burden in the present—that the God of Hope may give us grace to be found always and at the end working with faith and courage in the forefront of our opportunity.

APPENDICES

APPENDIX A

The Translation of Ephesians v. 16.—In his recent invaluable edition of the Epistle to the Ephesians, the Dean of Westminster says: "There seems to be no authority for interpreting the word (ἐξαγοραζόμενοι) as 'to buy up'"—the interpretation given by the Revised Version in the margin, and adopted by the Bishop of Birmingham in his commentary on the epistle. The Dean gives good grounds for his judgment; but the general sense of the passage remains the same. As he expresses it: "The Apostle appears to be urging his readers to claim the present for the best uses. It has got, so to speak, into wrong hands—they must purchase it out of them for themselves." Again, "The wise may ransom the time from loss or misuse, release it from the bondage of the evil and claim it for the highest good. . . . There is a Divine Purpose working for good in the midst of evil; the children of light can perceive it and follow its guidance." I have, therefore, throughout the lectures made frequent use of the phrase, "buying up the opportunity," though it may strictly be not so much a translation of the Greek word as an extension of the meaning latent in St. Paul's advice.

APPENDIX B

A Future Use for Church Schools.—It is not within the purpose of the present volume to discuss, even indirectly, the future of Voluntary Elementary Schools. So long as the present Education Act remains in force, it is the duty of church-people to make every effort to maintain Church Schools. But for special reasons in many cases this is impossible; and in any case it is well to face the possibilities of the future. It is, therefore, worth while to insist that the educational policy of the Church is not restricted to the limits of Elementary "non-Provided Schools." If and when these cannot be retained, the premises remain stamped with an educational trust, and ought to be used for educational purposes. The Board of Education, as is well known, acting under the powers given to it under the Charitable Trusts Acts, is prepared to sanction schemes which provide that the premises shall be used for purposes which, however parochial or recreative, have still an educational character. It is here that the Church has a real opportunity. It may still use its school buildings to carry on educational work in a religious spirit by providing not only the usual Sunday-school, but classes and lectures in all sorts of subjects for lads and girls, young men and young women. For many of these, Government grants may be earned. If the State is wise, it will encourage efforts towards the continuation of education made by those who are in close touch with the children after they have left the Elementary Schools.

APPENDIX C

The London Religious Census.—The main results of the census are thus given in Mr. Mudie Smith's most instructive volume on "The Religious Life of London," p. 17. "Combining the results for London and Greater London, we find that the total population is 6,240,336 exclusive of those dwelling in institutions. The combined attendances (at places of worship) amount to 1,514,025, giving a ratio of 1 in every 4·11 of the population. The average of those attending a place of worship twice on a Sunday . . . is 38 per cent; this reduces the total of 1,514,025 (attendances), to 1,252,433 worshippers, giving a ratio of 1 in 5 of the population. In other words, four persons out of every five not dwelling in institutions, are either careless or hostile as regards public worship."

APPENDIX D

Associations of Visitors among the Poor.—An attempt has been made to "unite all visitors and workers among the poor in the Borough of Stepney into an Association, with a twofold purpose—first, that the individual knowledge and experience which visitors have gained might thus become more available for the common good ; and, secondly, that lectures might be provided by which instruction might be given to visitors, and the efficiency of the work in which they are engaged might be further increased. The Association consists of units made up of bodies of visitors directed by one head or accustomed to work together. Thus each group of workers attached to the different churches, missions, and settlements within the Borough forms a unit.

" The Association acts through these groups, and, as far as possible, in the place where their ordinary visitors' meetings are held. By this means it is hoped to meet the difficulty of those who hesitate to adopt a new organization in addition to those in operation. The objects of the Association in thus co-operating with the bodies of visitors are :—

"(1) To provide short talks with discussion on subjects of interest, to the visitors in their work, at their ordinary meetings—as, for example, such subjects as the prevention of infant mortality, the laws affecting tenant and lodger, the Factory Acts, the promotion of thrift, the laws of sanitation.   (2) To provide literature such as that issued by the National Health Society, for the visitors within the homes of those whom they visit, if they think fit.   (3) To commend to visitors through their Head special cases treated at the hospitals in regard to which the physicians desire to be assured that their instructions are being carried out in the home.   (4) To attempt a systematic visitation of the children about to leave school with a view to persuade them to join Thrift Societies, and to help them with information how best to do so.   (5) From time to time to get from the visitors information of general value which they have a unique opportunity of acquiring, e.g. the likelihood of special distress in their district, the extent of overcrowding, cases of defective sanitary arrangements, etc."

APPENDIX E

Religious Education of the Children of the Educated Classes.—The following extracts are taken from the Report of the Committee appointed by the Bishop of London, by desire of the Diocesan Conference, 1904, on "Religious Teaching and Influence among children and young people of higher education."

"A careful study of all the available evidence leads the Committee to conclude that there is growing up a great body of children who know very little of the Bible, who are not instructed in the Church Catechism, and are sadly ignorant of the Prayer Book and Church History. Some of these children in a few years will fill the foremost positions in the State, and be the leaders of Society. Their influence must be strong and far-reaching, and unless a change takes place, and takes place soon, in their early training, there is very little hope that that influence will be thrown upon the side of religion. . . .

"Nothing can be more painfully significant than the contrast between the care bestowed upon the secular education of the children of the upper classes, and the neglect of all really religious teaching. The testimony of clergy and teachers alike proves beyond any possibility of question that the religious knowledge of these children in the diocese is seriously and generally deficient. Many have expressed their thankfulness that the matter is receiving the attention of the Bishop.

"The causes which have led to this reach far down into the religious and social life of the upper classes.

The Committee are clear that the fault does not lie mainly in the great public schools, and not *primarily* with schools at all. . . .

"They note with thankfulness the improvement in the religious influence in public schools, and feel that in very many cases all that is practicable is being done. The failure is in the home, and with the parents. . . .

"There is a tendency among many really religious people to be content with the moralities of the Gospel without firm hold of the great doctrinal verities, which are the only permanent basis of Christian morals. They use the spiritual beauty of Christianity to appeal to the heart of a child, but forget that it will affect the child's life permanently only in so far as it is shown to rest on historic facts, and to possess Divine Authority.

"The Committee have already referred to the good work done in the great public schools. They thankfully recognize the admirable religious training and the definite spiritual influence of some other secondary schools. Yet, while there are not many that are wholly without religious instruction, the evidence before them shows that, in the large majority of schools where higher education is given, religious teaching is not given a prominent place.

"It consists generally of reading (with explanation) the historical books of the Bible, mainly those of the Old Testament. The instruction is rarely definite or dogmatic, except in a few church schools. . . .

"Many have pointed out that, though it is admitted that the religious knowledge of the children of the educated classes in this diocese is seriously deficient, yet the clergy as a whole are not alive to the gravity of this fact. The Committee fear this is so. Though there are many exceptions, in most parishes little is being done to give educated children systematic Bible teaching, and still less to impart knowledge of the Prayer Book and Church History.

"There may be something lacking, too, in the systematic instruction of their congregations by the clergy —failure, in fact, of the teaching office of the Church. Parents who have little idea of, or interest in, the Christian Faith as a body of truth, will see no reason for, and will take no interest in, teaching it in this aspect to their children.

"While children's services are general, there is often want of coherence and system in them, and absence of devices for enlisting the co-operation of the children. There is often failure to provide special facilities for the children of the upper classes when the ordinary ministrations fail to reach them."

APPENDIX F

A Men's Service in Bethnal Green.—For an account of a very remarkable Men's Service in East London, I may refer to the paper by the Rev. J. E. Watts Ditchfield, in " The Religious Life of London," edited by Mr. R. Mudie Smith (Hodder and Stoughton). Mr. Ditchfield's service at St. James-the-Less, Bethnal Green, has been the pivot round which the restoration of religious life in the parish has turned. I select one or two extracts from his paper which may serve both to emphasize some of the remarks in the text, and to suggest other possible lines of work. " If the men's service is to succeed, it must be the men's own service and not the parson's. Its basis should be democratic in the right sense of the word. The Committee number over seventy, and this large Committee is divided into sub-committees having charge of some department of work. The clergyman in charge must sink the parson in the man, and the more he is the man the more he will be the parson. He must set everybody to work, and be the example of every one in work."

"A very popular feature at my own service has been the putting of questions in boxes at the doors of the church. These once in six weeks have been taken into the pulpit and answered, instead of an address." [By this means, Mr. Ditchfield aims at avoiding the nuisance of the few "who talk for the sake of talking." It is an alternative to my own plan stated in the text, which some may prefer.]

"The man who puts children first will fail in two ways. He will not reach men, neither will he be likely to largely retain children as they grow up, for the lack of men in church will have convinced the children (while they are children) that it is unmanly to go to church. On the other hand, if he gets the men *they* will see that the children attend Sunday-school, who in their turn will be more likely to become churchgoers as they grow older."

As to the results of the service, which has 1,200 men on the roll, he says: "It has done much for the Church. It has broken down prejudice. It has increased the attendance at the ordinary services, and this very largely. It has influenced the work among women, and more especially among children. A women's service in church on Monday evenings numbering over 800 members, a Sunday-school with over 1,400 children, and a young men's Bible-class of over 260, show the influence of men attending church. It has reared for the Church real workers. Ninety per cent of our male workers are the result of this service. Many men come forward for confirmation. The number of communicants increased from 26 in 1897, to 597 in 1903 on Easter Day."

APPENDIX G

Sunday Services in Town Parishes.—It may well be doubted whether in our town parishes we have as yet succeeded in obtaining an ideal plan for the church-life on the Lord's Day—alike suited to the social conditions of the people and faithful to the true principles of Christian worship.

(1) Among all sections of churchpeople there is a growing desire to give to the Lord's Service, the Holy Communion, the place on the Lord's Day which it never ought and was never meant to have lost, as the principal act of the worship of the faithful.

(2) It can never rightly have this place unless and until there is one great parish communion every Sunday in which the aspect of the fellowship of the Body can be realized—the common sacrificial Meal, if one may with reverence so describe it, of the Household of God.

(3) It is difficult to realize this aspect if the hour be so early that it involves a real loss of that rest which our working people sorely need on the rest day, or so

late that only a very few can communicate. (I do not here discuss the question of the modern evening communion.)

(4) I cannot but think that if a real effort were made to have the parish communion at, say, 9 o'clock, or even 9.30, these difficulties might be largely overcome.

Is it not possible that the best Sunday scheme for a town parish would be something of this sort : (*a*) *The* "Divine Service" with every assistance which simple reverent congregational music can give at 9 or 9.30 a.m. (preceded by Morning Prayer as the Prayer Book contemplates, or in the case of older churches followed by it) as the great gathering of the Christian Body : (*b*) in the afternoon (after Sunday-school) the catechising in church, at which not only children but parents should be encouraged to be present ; and (*c*) preceded by Evening Prayer for such as desire it, in the evening the Service for the People, to which all sorts and conditions could come, and at which the main features would be simple prayer, the sermon, and many hymns.

I venture to suggest that this is the sort of Sunday in church to which truer conception of worship, a readier recognition of the missionary duty of the Church in the large towns, and the altered habits of life among the people, all seem to point.

APPENDIX H

United Evangelistic Effort.—In the Diocese of London the Bishop has appointed a permanent Council to stimulate and supervise the evangelistic work of the Church throughout the Diocese. After much careful inquiry it has decided to take certain large halls — such as town-halls, and even music-halls — in selected districts for special Mission Services, in which the church in the various neighbouring parishes will concentrate their efforts. It is too early to estimate the permanent result ; but at least as regards the numbers of non-churchgoing people who have attended the first experiments have been very encouraging. It need scarcely be pointed out that it is essential to the success of such ventures—(*a*) that the churches in any selected areas have the zeal, the efficiency, and the workers necessary to promote the central services, and still more, to follow them up ; and (*b*) that the clergy and other workers of these parishes are carefully consulted, and their hearty co-operation in every possible way secured.

Attention ought also to be called to the very remarkable effort made in the summer of 1905 by the Church in Blackpool, under the personal leadership of the Bishop of Manchester, to reach the masses of holiday folk. The Bishop's own account of the effort and of its results will be found in the " Guardian " of September 6th, 1905. It was a remarkable instance of the power which can be generated and the impression which can be produced by the Church acting as a united missionary body.

APPENDIX I

The Church of England Men's Society ("*C.E.M.S.*")
was formed only five years ago by Archbishop Temple,
as a means of federating and concentrating men's work
in the Church of England.   Its first chairman was the
present Bishop of London, to whom the writer of these
pages succeeded in 1901.   It consists of—(*a*) Members
who shall be communicants ; (*b*) Associates who shall
be professing members of the Church of England or of
the Churches in communion therewith, who accept the
Society's Rule of Life.   That Rule of Life, binding alike
on members and associates, is simple, but fundamental
—to pray to God every day, and to do something to
help forward the work of the Church.   The Society
aims—in the words of its last report—at "the building
up of bodies of loyal and zealous Churchmen linked
with one another throughout all the parishes of the
Empire."   It is thus not so much a new Society as an
effort to unite and inspire with a common enthusiasm
for the work of God isolated guilds and societies of
men.   Believing that it represents a spiritual cause, it
is deliberately flexible in its organization ; so that any
body of really zealous Churchmen in any parish or
diocese who accept the Rule of Life can be joined on
to it.   Its object is to prevent keen men from working
for their own parish only, or for some single bit of
work within their parish, but to make them realize that
they are comrades in a great movement throughout the
whole Church.

The Archbishop of Canterbury has written :—"Most

cordially do I commend the Society to the interest, the prayers, and the support of Churchmen." Speaking as President of the Society at a great gathering of its members in October, 1905, he said, after describing the widespreading problems with which as Archbishop he was inevitably concerned : "It is from this standpoint that I stand here to tell you that what you are doing—what *we* are doing—is, it seems to me, the very thing that is needed at this hour." Again, "I desire to bid you realize that at this juncture not England only, not our Empire only, but Christ's Church throughout the world wants you . . . as men with arms bared to the elbow, and loins girt for service, going out to fight against those things which are unworthy of that great Society, and which are staining and sullying our Christian life, and waiting to be trodden under foot, with God's help, by just the sort of Society that is banded together in this hall to-night."

The Bishop of London, at the Weymouth Church Congress, expressed the hope that a branch of the C.E.M.S. would be formed in every parish in the kingdom. It has been warmly taken up in South Africa and other parts of the empire, and no one can meet with its members, as the present writer has done in every part of England, without being convinced that if only it be true to its own spirit it may become a real power in bringing to English Churchmen the sense of a brotherhood of life and service.

Full information may always be obtained from the Secretary, Church House, Westminster, S.W.

APPENDIX K

A Parochial Church Council.—In the large parish of Portsea, with its population of over 45,000 people, the parish church and each of the mission churches had and still have an elected Church Council. The voters were communicants of full age of both sexes, who signed a declaration that they had communicated at the church at least three times during the previous year. Candidates were duly nominated at least a week before the election, their names posted on the church doors, and printed on the day of the election on a voting-paper. The election took place by ballot at stated hours during the day. Women were eligible for election, but not more than one third of the total number of members elected were allowed to be women. Careful rules were adopted as to the nature of the Council's business, and as to the manner of its transaction. It was expressly laid down that the Councils had no concern with doctrinal matters, and that any resolutions on ceremonial matters would be carefully considered, but were not binding. On other matters, as to hours of service, finance, special enterprises, etc., their advice was always followed. Each separate council elected delegates to form a General Parish Council, which dealt with matters affecting the parish as a whole. The number of persons who voted, in spite of the novelty of the experiment, compared favourably with ordinary civil local elections. These details are mentioned not because they represent an ideal system, or because they could be everywhere followed, but simply as showing the lines on which—in this case certainly without any friction or trouble—the experiment of a system of parochial representative Councils can be made.

PLYMOUTH
WILLIAM BRENDON AND SON, LTD.
PRINTERS

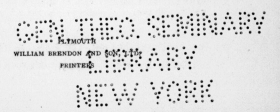

SELECT LIST OF NEW BOOKS

Principles of Parish Work : an Essay in Pastoral Theology. By the Rev. CLEMENT F. ROGERS, M.A. Crown 8vo, 5s. net.

Pastoral Work in Country Districts. Lectures delivered in the Divinity School at Cambridge, Lent, 1905. By the Rev. V. S. S. COLES, M.A., Principal of the Pusey House, Oxford. Crown 8vo.

Pastors and Teachers : Six Lectures on Pastoral Theology. Delivered in the Divinity School, Cambridge, in the year 1902. By the Right Rev. EDMUND ARBUTHNOTT KNOX, D.D., Bishop of Manchester. With an Introduction by the Right Rev. CHARLES GORE, D.D., Bishop of Birmingham. Crown 8vo, 5s. net.

CHEAP EDITION. Without the Appendices. Crown 8vo, 1s. net.

The Church and the Nation : Charges and Addresses. By MANDELL CREIGHTON, D.D., sometime Bishop of London. Crown 8vo, 5s. net.

The Personal Life of the Clergy. By the Rev. ARTHUR W. ROBINSON, B.D. Crown 8vo, 2s. 6d. net. (*Handbooks for the Clergy.*)

The Ministry of Conversion. By the Rev. A. J. MASON, D.D., Master of Pembroke College, Cambridge. Crown 8vo, 2s. 6d. net. (*Handbooks for the Clergy.*)

Pastoral Visitation. By the Rev. H. E. SAVAGE, M.A., Vicar of Halifax. Crown 8vo, 2s. 6d. net. (*Handbooks for the Clergy.*)

LONGMANS, GREEN, & CO.

LONDON, NEW YORK, AND BOMBAY